Lesbian, Queer, and Bisexual Women in Heterosexual Relationships

Lesbian, Queer, and Bisexual Women in Heterosexual Relationships

Narratives of Sexual Identity

Ahoo Tabatabai

LEXINGTON BOOKS
Lanham • Boulder • New York • London

Published by Lexington Books
An imprint of The Rowman & Littlefield Publishing Group, Inc.
4501 Forbes Boulevard, Suite 200, Lanham, Maryland 20706
www.rowman.com

Unit A, Whitacre Mews, 26-34 Stannary Street, London SE11 4AB

Copyright © 2016 by Lexington Books

All rights reserved. No part of this book may be reproduced in any form or by any electronic or mechanical means, including information storage and retrieval systems, without written permission from the publisher, except by a reviewer who may quote passages in a review.

British Library Cataloguing in Publication Information Available

Library of Congress Cataloging-in-Publication Data

Tabatabai, Ahoo, 1978– author.
Lesbian, queer, and bisexual women in heterosexual relationships : narratives of sexual identity / Ahoo Tabatabai.
p. cm.
Includes bibliographical references and index.
ISBN 978-1-4985-0561-1 (cloth : alk. paper) – ISBN 978-1-4985-0562-8 (ebook)
1. Lesbians–Identity. 2. Lesbians–Relations with heterosexuals. 3. Lesbians–Sexual behavior. 4. Bisexual women–Identity. 5. Bisexual women–Sexual behavior. 6. Heterosexuality. I. Title.
HQ75.5.T33 2016
306.76'63–dc23
2015030611

∞™ The paper used in this publication meets the minimum requirements of American National Standard for Information Sciences Permanence of Paper for Printed Library Materials, ANSI/NISO Z39.48-1992.

Printed in the United States of America

Contents

Acknowledgments	vii
Introduction: Born This Way	ix
1 Narratives	1
2 Appearance	11
3 Not Bisexual	23
4 Not Lesbian	37
5 Not Straight	45
6 Hetero-cash	65
Conclusion: Self and Story-Telling	77
Bibliography	87
Index	93
About the Author	95

Acknowledgments

I would like to thank all the women who took the time to share their stories with me. I would like to extend a special thanks to Annulla Linders, Steve Carlton-Ford, Rhys Williams, Erynn Masi de Casanova, and Julie Hilvers for their comments on earlier drafts of this manuscript. I would like to thank Lexington Books, and particularly Brighid Stone, Jana Hodges-Kluck, and Joseph Parry, for their interest in this project. Finally, I'd like to thank my partner, Shane, and my son, Kaveh, for their continued love and support.

Introduction

Born This Way

With the increased visibility of the marriage equality movement, it seems that discussions of sexuality are more public than ever. These discussions rest on basic normative assumptions about sexuality. Most people use the term "sexual orientation" to distinguish heterosexuals from bisexuals and homosexuals. Most people also assume that sexual orientation is a stable individual trait, one that is either a biological predisposition or set in early life. The question of the origin of sexual orientation is highly politicized. Sexual orientation, as a stable feature, one that a person is perhaps even born with, is part of the framing of the current gay rights activism, including the movement for marriage equality. In order to counter the religious right's argument that gays and lesbians don't deserve equal rights because they are making a choice to be gay, hence the terminology of "sexual preference," some advocates have chosen to argue that homosexuality is inborn. Although this may have been an effective political strategy in the past (some would argue that it was never an effective strategy[1]), this line of thinking has reinforced the assumptions that "real" sexuality is stable and unchanging. Within this framework, arguing from the standpoint of a biologically determined sexual orientation is the only legitimate basis for combatting discrimination. By extension, only those whose sexuality is thought to be biologically determined, thus unchangeable, deserve protection under the law. But this is not the only way that one might think about sexuality. Another perspective posits that sexuality is shaped by society and is not solely biologically determined. Sexuality, all sexuality, is social (Plummer 2003). People build who they are, including who they are sexually, through experiencing various events and interpreting those experiences. Although there may be limited space to do so within the current political framework, to say that sexual identity is not biologically determined in no way implies that it is not socially significant. Sexual identity, whether biological or social, can be the basis for the formation of families and communities and it can also be the basis for discrimination. It is not biology that makes sexual identity socially significant. Sexual identity, along with race, class, gender, and a number of other traits, not only shape personal experience but they are also features of social hierarchies.

There is a social difference, for example, between someone who understands herself as lesbian and someone who considers herself straight. This distinction can become the basis for the formation of two communities. This border, although not grounded in biological/genetic differences, is socially important. At a basic level, it can determine access to certain resources, like the legal recognition of a relationship. Defining who one is sexually is not an individual project. It is a social project, where individuals are accountable to others and are themselves shaped by social institutions. As with any identity, there are meanings and social expectations associated with sexual identities. Even an understanding of sexuality that moves away from biological determinism has to account for these meanings and expectations. Examining individual sexual accounts, or narratives, allows not only for an understanding of individuals' sense of who they are, but also the ways in which a given society organizes sexuality.

This book examines the identity narratives of 32 women who once identified as lesbian, bisexual, or queer and subsequently partnered with men, with the goal of understanding who they believe themselves to be and how they engage with social expectations associated with their old and new identities.

DEMOGRAPHIC CHARACTERISTICS OF PARTICIPANTS

Age:
Mean = 30 years
Range = 22–43 years

Race/ethnicity:
White/Caucasian (20), Multi-racial (7), Other (3), Black/African American (2)

Educational attainment:
Master's (11), Some college (9), Bachelor's (7), Doctorate (2), High school diploma (1)

Sexual identity:
Bisexual (11), Queer (7), No-label (3), Straight (2), Bi-queer (2), Lesbian (1), Dyke (1), Pansexual (1), Fluid (1), Queer-Lesbian (1), Married (1)

It might be tempting to assume that all these women might identify as bisexual. In fact, they do not. For the most part, they also do not identify as heterosexual or lesbian. And yet, this book is not about why some lesbians date men and some do not, rather it is about how the crossing of a symbolic boundary is navigated, managed, and, in some cases, challenged. These are not only stories about an individual experience of change, but they are also stories that highlight cultural definitions associated with sexuality and bring to light the basis for communal belonging. The focus of this book is on how identity narratives are constructed. In the process, the narratives highlight what social assumptions still shape discussions of sexuality.

NARRATING IDENTITIES

Telling the story of one's self is a performance of identity. Like any other performance, constructing these stories requires scripts. Also like other performances, this construction happens on a "stage," as these stories are not created in a vacuum. I will come back to the concept of stage, but I'd like to begin by examining the notion of narrative scripts.

Scripts

Narratives are not objective accounts of "actual" events. Analysis of narratives is not the way to uncover whatever one may consider "what really happened." Narratives are interesting and rich precisely because they bring subjectivity into focus. Often, narratives of identity require scripts. Scripts should not be understood in the literal sense of words to be memorized, but as a way to organize ideas in recognizable ways. How should a story be told? If an individual joins a self-aware community, the community itself provides the individual with ways to make sense of their experience. Twelve-step programs, for example, invite participants to think of their addictions as powerful forces that control their lives. This is a form of a script that allows new members to understand, articulate, and perform their identity.

Not surprisingly, leaving a community offers ex-members fewer options, or scripts, to make sense of their exit than does joining one. Women who identified as lesbian, bisexual, or queer and subsequently partner with men do not enter a new community with specific scripts. It is true that when they partnered with men they may have been read as heterosexual, but it is difficult to imagine what one might call a heterosexual community, in the sense of a community organized in a self-aware manner around the identity of heterosexual. It is doubtful that the women would want to be part of such a community even if it did exist. They have to find their own way of making sense of what is happening. In essence, they have to piece together their own scripts. Circumstances that lead to "leaving" a community no doubt impact the narrative. But these women did not really leave "lesbianism" because they found it dissatisfying. They didn't consciously leave it at all. They made a choice, partnering with a man, and that choice moved them across a symbolic community boundary. Constructing these narratives is part of their identity work.

THE STAGE

It is true that on an individual level, one might consider each conversation its own stage and each conversation partner an audience. But the stage that I wish to focus on is the cultural backdrop to the discussion of sexual identity. The current cultural and political environment serves as a frame for narratives of sexuality. Some key elements of this cultural and political framing are worth highlighting. One feature is the above-mentioned assumption that "real" sexuality has biological roots. The second feature, clearly related to the first, is that gender is the basis for the sexual classification of individuals. The consensus seems to be that it is by virtue of matching one's gender with the gender of one's subject of interest that a person comes to be read as heterosexual, bisexual, and homosexual. In very meaningful ways, the notion of a queer sexuality challenges this very assumption. However, it is not (yet) part of the dominant cultural and political backdrop of the discussion of sexuality.

A final feature, an extension of the gendered organization, is that sexual activity is central to sexual identity. But as this book will show, engaging in sexual behavior with a member of the same or other gender is not a prerequisite for identifying in a particular way. While behavior has a place in discussions of sexuality, so do desire and identity. For some individuals, behavior may be central to their sense of sexual self. For others, desire can exist without the corresponding behavior. It is possible that a woman who used to be involved with other women and now with a man, would choose to not change her sexual identity, because behavior is not the basis for her sexual identification. Her desire for women, if it still exists, may still be the most important feature of her understanding of her sexual self. Certain acts may have existed for centuries, but associating acts with the people who perform them is a fairly new organization. Even today, there are well-documented cases of cultures in which the notion of homosexual and heterosexual do not resemble the Western organization.

Introduction xiii

THE UNMARKED

Many of the women whose accounts I present could recall a traditional process of coming out to family and friends as lesbian, queer, or bisexual. Although the shift to a male partner could be seen as a coming-out of sorts, in important ways it is different from the "classic" coming-out. For one, these women's experiences can be understood as moving away from an identity that is still stigmatized to one where there is an opportunity to experience less stigma. After having lived most of their lives within a "marked" category–lesbian, queer, bisexual–the women interviewed for this study suddenly found themselves in an "unmarked" category, once they entered into relationships with men—straight or heterosexual. Far from experiencing the transition from marked to unmarked as a relief, as might be expected, for some the invisibility associated with being unmarked was neither expected nor welcome; in fact, for some, it brought a sense of discomfort. And so, some try to renegotiate a marked identity for themselves but one that is different from their previous lesbian/bisexual/queer identity. In other words, the women are struggling to be read as non-straight to themselves as well as to others, despite living lives that had all the outward trappings of straightness (I will discuss this in depth in chapter 6). Their goal is not necessarily to be read as something, but specifically to not be read as straight. In this sense, their struggles are the reverse of the better-documented struggles of people who for various reasons seek to achieve the kind of invisibility that comes with an unmarked identity. If the move from an unmarked to a marked category is conceptualized as parallel to the move from a marked to unmarked category, then the same theoretical tools that have guided studies documenting the former transition should be useful for the latter as well. But there are good reasons to assume that some theoretical elaboration is necessary to understand how the women accomplish this non-straight identity. The women who leave female partners to begin relationships with male partners have the capacity to redefine their sexual identity. But their capacity for such a creative process is limited. There are few stories that can serve as guides for how this coming-out story can be told, because in reality this change is very different from the more common coming-out stories. The women's task is to negotiate the legitimacy of their current choices (being with men) with their previous choices (being with women). In the process of framing their decision in a way that renders their claim to a stable identity as legitimate, the women communicate their understandings of notions of community and belonging. They also show a nuanced regard for sexual categories. They stretch the boundaries of some categories, while preserving and even policing the boundaries of other categories.

WHERE ARE THEY?

It is difficult to find people who are no longer part of a defined community. This was one of the major difficulties of recruiting participants for this study. Since the labels the women used to define themselves was part of the matter under investigation, the task was made even more difficult. Where would one post a notice seeking participants? I had to find a way of defining the criteria for inclusion clearly enough so as to gain access, but I could not make a selection based on a particular identity outcome. I couldn't ask for participation from "bisexual women" or "lesbians" since I did not want to make assumptions about what language would actually be specific enough to invite the people I was interested in. I settled on a call that asked for the participation of women who in their life have identified as lesbian, queer, or bisexual and who now predominately engage in relationships with men.

I first requested to interview women whom I knew (4 out of the 32 participants). Once interviewed, those women contacted women that they knew who would fit the interview criteria. In addition I asked two online lesbian and bisexual organizations to post a notice about my study on their websites and/or listservs. One of those organizations refused to do so, because they understood the purpose of my work as being one that advocates that lesbians can become straight if they choose to. Despite lengthy explanations of my intentions, they refused to post my notice. This concern was brought up again by one of the women that I interviewed. Hope mentioned that before coming to the interview, she had been warned by a friend to be cautious, thinking that it was possible that my purpose was to recruit people for some type of lesbian "rehabilitation" program. The difficulty in locating these women may explain why only a handful of studies have been conducted about their experiences.

Before each interview began, I explained the purpose of the research to the women. I did not however, share any details about my own partnership status or sexual identity. After the interview, I invited the women to ask me any question that they wished. The women had self-selected into the study, but I still felt that after having shared what for some was a private narrative, they should have the opportunity to ask me the same questions I had asked of them. As mentioned, some of the women were already familiar with my relationship status and sexual identity, since they were friends or acquaintances. Women whom I did not know often did take the opportunity to ask me why I was interested in this topic as opposed to another. I responded to their questions candidly. The only noticeable difference between women who knew me and those who didn't was in the use of some phrases throughout the interview. Women who knew me were more likely to end their assertions with "You know what I mean!?!" while women who did not know me personally were more likely to end with "Does this make sense?" None of the women are identified by their real name. I offered each woman the opportunity to choose her own alias. Some did so. Other aliases were assigned by me.

OVERVIEW

In this book, I examine how the participants construct coherent stories about choosing to be with a partner of different gender with the goal of presenting how social expectations are incorporated into individual narratives. Narratives that organize life events into a coherent picture are necessary in order to maintain a stable picture of the self. The seemingly contradictory experiences of being attracted to both women and men are woven into the narrative. This narrative serves as the means through which the socially unmarked identity is "done."

Chapter 1 presents the women's own accounts of how this change happened. The chapter focuses on the ways the story of involvement with men is told. I outline several strategies the women use to produce narratives. I show how the narrative itself is part of their identity work. The chapter is organized around the key themes of the narratives.

Chapter 2 also examines ways of telling this story, but this time through appearance, focusing on how the women use their appearance to further challenge or reinforce assumptions about their sexual identity.

Chapter 3 presents an engagement with the label of bisexual. Many people assume that the women in question are bisexual because they have partnered with both women and men. This chapter shows a more complicated picture. The women are not generally fond of the label of bisexual. They find that the negative baggage that the label carries (namely that bisexual people are fickle or untrustworthy) make it undesirable.

Chapter 4 addresses the reasons why the women choose not to call themselves lesbians anymore. Only two of the 32 women use the label to describe themselves. This is not because they don't like the label or because they think that they are not lesbian. The reasons have more to do with respect for the lesbian community than with a sense of dissatisfaction with that label.

Chapter 5 explores the issues around the rejection of the label "straight." The women reject the label of "straight" or "heterosexual," but they also reject "bisexual" and lesbian. The reasons for rejecting straight are very different from those for rejecting "lesbian." Whereas rejection of lesbian has to do with protecting the authenticity of the community to which they used to belong, the rejection of the label straight has to do with the invisibility of being in an unmarked category. The women do not think of themselves as "straight" women partially because they believe straight implies a certain gender order to which they do not subscribe.

Despite the rejection of the label "straight," the women are read as such. Being read as straight bestows on them and their relationships a certain level of privilege. Chapter 6 explores the ways the women engage with the benefits and privileges of being read as heterosexual. They share the ways that they try to counter the effect of heterosexism. Their main strategy is serving as allies to the LGBTQ communities.

SOME LIMITATIONS

People can only report what they can articulate. And people will tell the story that they are asked to tell. By virtue of inviting them to tell a particular story, I have already inserted myself in the story as a key player. As mentioned previously, I knew several of the women in the study personally. I worked to account for this fact.

Being a lesbian, bisexual, or queer woman in the United States is different than being lesbian, bisexual, or queer elsewhere in the world. Even in the context of the United States, being in the Midwest may give identities a different character than being in coastal cities, which are known for their large and visible LGBTQ populations. The visibility of an LGBTQ community may make certain scripts available, where they would not be available elsewhere. This fact certainly contributes to the limitations of this study. A preliminary study such as this can and should lead to further research that examines the impact that regionality can have on these particular identity processes.

A final note about language is important to keep in mind. The women shared their identities prior to partnering with men and after doing so. These categories should not be considered a "point a" to "point b," as the relationship between the two categories is not linear. As the book will show, for most of the participants these categories are place-holders, as they offer spaces from which to construct a narrative of self.

NOTE

1. See Suzanna Walters' essay, "The Power in 'Choosing to Be Gay'" in the June 3rd, 2014, issue of *The Atlantic*.

Chapter One

Narratives

Ask anyone how they came to have the career that they have, or how they came to give their child a particular name. What you get in response is a story. When people tell stories about their lives, they not only recount events that have taken place but they also in essence communicate who they are. Telling the story of one's identity is more significant than just accounting for facts.

These stories can be particularly important when trying to explain life changes, like leaving a career in finance to open a bakery. The story is also critical when events, like a change to a partner of a different gender, might lead to a change in identity. While it may be possible to justify being both a financier and a baker, in the current system of sexual classification, it is not possible to be both straight and gay. Homosexual and heterosexual are considered mutually exclusive. Even the Kinsey scale, often cited as a measure of fluid sexuality, places homosexual and heterosexual at the opposite ends of its continuum. Accounting for the transition from one end of the continuum to the other becomes the most important part of this story. My goal when speaking to these women was not to gauge the validity of their story—but to hear how they constructed the story itself—thus understanding who they understood themselves to be. The question of "how did this come to be," is really a question about what kind of person the women understand themselves to be.

When individuals tell stories, they rely on available cultural scripts in order to communicate elements that listeners will find recognizable and true. Scripts offer a way of making sense of events in a recognizable way, offering a frame for the individual process of accounting for identity and a glimpse into social guidelines associated with those identities. The financier turned baker, for example, may rely on scripts having to do with "finding one's passion," or "risking security for creativity."

How is the story of a lesbian in love with a man usually told? Ironically, this story is usually not told. There are not many stories readily available of lesbians dating men. The exception to this is found in a handful of Hollywood representations like the character of Tina on the Showtime series *The L-Word*, the 1997 film *Chasing Amy*, and a brief mention in the 1994 film *Go Fish* (which some women to whom I spoke coincidentally mention). Most of those references are not particularly flattering, as they paint such people as fickle, childish, and indecisive. Despite not having exact scripts to explain their life trajectory, the women use available scripts to piece together a story that authenticates their identity claim. In this chapter, I present the main scripts utilized for this purpose.

CLASSIC COMING-OUT

One available script is the "classic" coming-out story. By classic I mean here the experience of having gone from having a heterosexual identity (straight) to having a sexual minority identity (lesbian, bisexual, queer, etc.). The classic coming-out story usually begins with an individual's realization that they are attracted to people of the same gender. The process of coming out includes sharing that knowledge with one's self and with others. In some cases, it includes embracing a new sexual identity. Most women with whom I spoke experienced a classic coming-out. At one point in their life, they came out as bisexual, lesbian, dyke, and/or queer. It is not surprising then that some even begin the story of their attraction to men with their classic coming-out story. Some women explained that when they partnered with men and had to account for it, they experienced what could amount to a "reverse coming-out," or as Karen, one of the research participants, calls it, a "going back into the closet." Some women used elements of the classic coming-out story to establish this shift as a quasi-coming-out of its own. They recount stories of telling parents, friends, and coworkers. They expressed the need to be true to one's self regardless of others' feedback, as the following examples show.

> Owning attraction to men again, possibly not being with a woman, is consistent experientially with a lesbian coming out, with her being attracted to a woman in a culture that frowns on that. (Heather)

> Well, I came out as lesbian because I wasn't gonna let society define who it was ok for me to love, so, now what am I gonna decide is not ok? And so, I decided to go with it. But I kept it a secret for a good while. [She continued.] Most of my friends thought that I was joking at first, so they went through that

very typical when you come out to somebody phase of "hahahaha, yeah right, oh my god you're serious," kind of reaction. (Jennifer)

If it was a straight person coming out I would applaud them for doing what was right and following their attractions and why shouldn't I do that. (Karen)

We've gotten to the point where I was like "hey, by the way." So, it's almost like this whole coming out thing. Like, each time, it's like dropping a little bomb or whatever. (Margaret)

Jennifer draws a parallel between her experience of falling in love with a woman and with a man. By doing so, she reinforces the idea of a continuous identity. Her previous choice of being with a woman is presented as similar to the choice to be with a man. Karen similarly explains following one's attraction as "doing what was right," regardless of whether it is with a man or a woman.

The classic coming-out narrative is useful for these women, first, because it is a story with which they are familiar. Many have developed such accounts in the past. Second, the coming-out story, as a scenario, is culturally available to others, to the listeners. By saying that they experience something akin to coming-out, the women invite their listener to think of their story in terms that are similar to the classic coming-out story, that is, of having a true self and being honest with oneself and one's desires. But the coming-out story is not an entirely perfect fit. The classic coming-out implies that the current identity is the "real" identity, while their previous identity was misinformed. It creates a narrative through which the individual comes to embrace who they really are, despite its social cost. But this is not entirely the story that these women would like to tell. Their task is not simply to present a current, and previously denied true self, but instead to present both the past and the present as part of their true self. The classic coming-out story cannot deliver this on its own. Thus, although the women make references to the coming-out story, it is only one of the scripts they use to account for what happened.

THE PHASE

The coming-out story is limited in its ability to simultaneously authenticate both the past and present as true expressions of identity. These women use elements of the coming-out narrative but supplement it with other scripts. A second immediately available script is that of having gone through a phase. With this script, a temporary embrace of a sexual minority identity can easily be written off as having been "just a phase." Only two women, the only two women who identify as straight today used the phase script in an effort to account for their previous choices. I asked Jenny, a 29-year-old Iranian woman, if she ever thought about her involvement with women. She corrected me. She was involved with *a* woman. This distinction was important to her. I asked her if she ever thought about it and if so, what she would say about it today:

> Jenny: I wouldn't say I think about it on a daily basis but it does cross my mind, say once a month.
>
> Me: Can you think about what are those instances that make you think about it? Do you know what brings it up?
>
> Jenny: It doesn't have to be anything specific. I mean sometimes I just think "damn. I did that" you know.
>
> Me: And then what do you think?
>
> Jenny: I think [yelling] WHAT THE HELL WAS I THINKING?
>
> Me: Why?
>
> Jenny: Because I don't think even if I wanted to, I don't think I could sustain a relationship with a woman, a long-term relationship with a woman and be happy.

For Jenny, having once been with a woman is something that she cannot easily reconcile with her current sense of self. The best she can do, short of denying that the events ever took place, is to express her disbelief that she was once partnered with a woman. Denying her involvement with her female partner was not an available option for Jenny since she and her previous partner were my friends at the time. As I will explore further in other chapters, Jenny does deny or hide her previous experience when she has the opportunity to do so.

Although the other women with whom I spoke could have used the idea of a phase as Jenny did, they instead use it to accomplish a very different goal. First, they show their awareness of the script by stating that friends and family understood their experience as such.

> I sometimes felt a sort of eye rolling, like it was some sort of phase for me or something, or a novelty of some kind. (Amy)

> There was definitely a lot of joy from straight friends and family since they felt that I was settling down, I think. (laugh) The phase was over. (Celia)

But then, the women use this bit of information as a platform to show how their experience should precisely not be understood as a phase. Meg, a 30-year-old white woman, recalls her discomfort with the assumption:

> I think they feel, and not just like my parents, my extended family my grandma, grandpa, like we're talking and I'll be like "we're not in a monogamous relationship and I may still sleep with women" just because I want them to realize that this wasn't a phase and whatever.

Part of the identity work then becomes explaining exactly how something that could look like a phase is, in fact, not a phase. One way that the women do this is by acknowledging that some people do go through a phase, but that their own experience does not qualify as one. They work to distance themselves from, for example, what Alia, a 25-year-old Caucasian woman, calls BUGs.

> It stands for bi-until-graduation. Girls that experiment in college or they do it 'cause it turns guys on to make out with girls at parties and things like that, who aren't really attracted to women, they're sometimes called BUGs.

Using this scenario, Alia communicates that although she is involved with a man, her attraction to women is real and remains part of her life, and thus was not a phase. Although it is not used as a justification, elements of the phase script are used to explain what did not happen. Some accounts are explicitly anti-phase, as in Meg's case. Even those who do not explicitly reference the phase do engage with it by working to show that their desire to be with a man was unexpected. The phase is explained away by highlighting the ways in which the attraction, encounter, and involvement with men was unintentional or "just happened."

THE ACCIDENT

In order to show that the choice to be with men, as Anne, a 28-year-old white woman, puts it "just fell together," it is essential to show that the current choice happened *involuntarily*. The assumption here is that partnering with women was fulfilling and sufficient and could have been maintained voluntarily indefinitely. As Margaret puts it: "I didn't go out to a bar looking for a guy. I bumped into a guy while I was out. If I bumped into a woman while I was out, I'd be dating a woman right now." Tina, a 38-year-old white woman, simply adds: "Ah, yeah. It was total accident."

> I don't know how it happened. It just kinda happened. I don't know if he tripped and fell into me. I don't know. Nothing like that has ever happened, it just did. (Ayana)

Even though Ayana's explanation speaks to a concrete, physical encounter, she still maintains that she doesn't know how exactly it came about. It is as if the attraction had caught her by surprise. Heather and Jenny echo a similar point.

> I think it just kinda came up and I noticed that I was having responses, like I was attracted again, like the goofy smile or the blushing, or the joking a little bit or the heart rate speeding up a little bit. (Heather)

> You know, it just happened. I mean, like I said I wasn't looking to date anyone. I wasn't thinking about dating. We met. We talked. He asked me out on a date. I was so excited, like I was jumping up and down when he sent me that email and that was it. There is no thought going into it. (Jenny)

Jennifer explains that she was herself unaware of her attraction to her male partner, until a friend pointed it out.

> I mean that's the reason that I didn't tell people for a long time. I felt horrible about it and like I said if I had been really conscious of what was happening, I wouldn't have let myself fall in love with him in the first place. I didn't want to date a man.

To say their involvement with men was an accident, or just happened, or just fell together, takes agency away from the women themselves and places it on circumstance. The women construct themselves as innocent bystanders, as the term "accident" clearly indicates. Saying that the event was an accident implies several other things. Notably, it implies that sexuality, or attraction, is a drive, in the Freudian sense, that it is a force within the individual that cannot be controlled. Further, the assumption is that entering into a relationship with someone based on that attraction is a valid decision. The involvement could have easily been with another woman as Margaret states. But by chance, it was with a man. Framing the events as having occurred outside of the given woman's control is an extremely effective way of authenticating both past and present identities.

Beth, a 30-year-old white woman, for example, states that "it was one of those things that like happened so fast, I didn't even know what happened." Ari, a 27-year-old white Jewish woman, insists:

> I don't know it was just one of those things, you know, you're out having fun one night and you're like, start hanging out with them and it wasn't like calculated or anything.

The statements have two outcomes. First, the assumption becomes that the previous identity was fulfilling and valid, true and real, until something unexpected happened outside of the woman's control and second, that there was no intention of moving away from dating women.

THE PERSON

Another powerful way of framing their experience is by arguing that gender is not an organizing feature of their attraction. This argument is hard to maintain since socially there is no denying that homophobia contributes to making a heterosexual relationship easier to manage publicly than a lesbian relationship. (I will discuss the women's engagement with the notion of privilege in Chapter 6.) As Emily, a 32-year-old white woman, states: "it's socially easier to be in a straight relationship." The social perks, "hetero dollars" or "hetero cash" as Claire calls it, that accompany a heterosexual relationship are numerous. Jennifer confirms:

> A huge, huge amount of privilege. I can walk safely down the street with him. I don't hold his hand in public but I could if I wanted to and, without any fear whatsoever. I could walk around [the city] with absolute safety with my partner. Having kids is really really easy, (laugh) disturbingly easy. And you know, my kids don't have to answer questions about which one of us is their real parent. And, there's a huge amount of privilege that I gained.

Nala, a 22-year-old Greek-American woman, adds: "there are obvious privileges that come with it, like on a very, on like a very materialist mode of thinking. Life is easier for straight people."

But in order to maintain the authenticity of their identity, these social rewards cannot be counted as motivation for the attraction to men. The women, even those who are now straight, account for their relationships with men as a response to their desire and how they "really feel." Incidentally, these are also elements of the classic coming-out story. These women both acknowledge that heterosexual relationships come with institutional benefits and also stress that these benefits were not motivating factors in their attraction to men. The women also use a gender-blind script to account for their involvement with men. Framing attraction in this way enables the women to conclude that their attractions are not directed at men as men but instead at people who happen to be men. This subtle distinction is useful because it allows attraction to be given primary importance and thus the benefits that come with the men become secondary. The attraction is to the individual regardless of gender and the benefits that come with the gender are uninvited, unintentional, and—perhaps—not even noticed. In fact, Skyler, a 25-year-old Chinese woman, found herself unable to articulate any benefits of being in a heterosexual relationship. Others were able to name at least some benefits, such as more acceptance by colleagues and family members, ability to show affection in public, and even institutional benefits like marriage rights. All maintained, however, that the benefits are not motivation for having become involved with a man. Attraction to the person and not the gender divests the women from any social benefits that could potentially come with being in a heterosexual relationship.

> I felt like I found the right person and so, it, I mean, it's like it didn't matter the gender but it was with a guy and I knew that I wanted to be with him for the rest of my life and so that was kinda how the shift happened, it wasn't, it wasn't any like deliberate decision. (Abigail, 30, white)

In her short statement, Abigail simultaneously enacts the gender-blind and the just-happened scripts. She states that her being with a man was something that just happened and that gender was in fact not a feature of her attraction.

Pam explains that in the context of her job, she started wondering if being with a man would make work relationships easier to manage. She clarifies: "But it happened first, like the dating of men happened before the wondering." In other words, she restated that her motivation was not the benefit. The benefits of being with men have to be bracketed out of the equation when the story of attraction is told in order for the identity claim to remain authentic. In order for the women to state that they could have maintained relationships with female partners had they not accidentally met a man, they cannot allow the social benefits of being with a man to be seen as motivation for the choice. And the accidental nature of their involvement with men is crucial in maintaining the authenticity of their identity.

A subset of the person-not-gender justification is one that explains that this particular man is, as Anne put it, "just really different than most men."

> I don't think that could happen with another guy. So, it was really weird. So, guys in general I probably wouldn't go out with. He's just different. (Tina)

Jennifer echoes Tina's point, by claiming that her male partner is the only man "in the universe" with whom she would begin a relationship.

> It wasn't that I just hadn't met the right man yet. It's that I just happened to meet the only man in the universe that would be interesting to me.

Jennifer adds that her attraction was to her partner and not to men. She adds: "I almost never notice men as attractive." Telling the story in this way accounts for her attraction to men and also helps maintain the authenticity of her previous identity. Very deliberately, the attraction is framed in terms of individuals. Benefits of heterosexuality do not depend on individual men, however. But framing attraction in terms of particular individuals creates further distance between the male-partner and a heterosexual relationship.

Some women went a step further and explained that their attraction to their male partners was similar if not identical to their attraction to women.

> I feel it necessary to explain why him and I always say "well, you know, it's not because he's a man. It's because of the characteristics that he has. He's very gentle and he's tiny and he's soft and the things that I like about him are the things that remind me of a woman." (Celia)

Not only is this man different, but he is also like a woman. If this man is like a woman, then it becomes less difficult to explain attraction to him while still maintaining the authenticity of attraction to women.

THE LOVE SCRIPT

When the women spoke of not having control over their attraction and following attraction into partnership, they rely on cultural scripts about romantic love that assert that one is powerless toward attraction and that sexual attraction is the basis for partnership (Swidler 2001).

One of the more common cultural love scripts is the notion of "love at first sight." By using such love scripts, the women are able to present their choice of being with men as one that is motivated by love as opposed to being motivated by the benefits of heterosexuality. Jenny recalls meeting her partner:

> You know, it just happened. I mean, like I said I wasn't looking to date anyone. I wasn't thinking about dating. We met. We talked. He asked me out on a date. I was so excited, like I was jumping up and down when he sent me that email and that was it. There is no thought going into it. There is no "oh wow. Oh my god. He's a guy." I was like "oh my god. Oh my god. He asked me out" . . . I was thinking like "oh my god. I think I'm in love with this guy and I kinda want to marry him." I hung up and I told my mom. "You know this guy. I don't know what he looks like. I don't know what kind of guy he is but just from his voice I can tell if we don't end up dating, we will be really good friends."

Jenny not only uses the "love at first sight" script, but she supplements it with the "love is blind" script. Love at first sight is a recognizable myth about the basis of partnership. It creates a scenario in which individuals are meant to be together and find each other against all odds. The implication is that the union was "always meant to be," taking agency away from the actors. Regardless of what their personal beliefs about love and romance are, the use of "love at first sight" is an effective way of explaining and justifying how they ended up with male partners.

Alia also uses culturally common notions of love to explain her decision to marry her male partner. Alia was married once before, prior to her involvement with her female partner. She then married a second time after that relationship ended.

> I knew I wanted to be with them forever, the two men that I married. It didn't work out with my first husband, but I knew that even though my current husband and I have an open relationship, I knew that I wanted to be with him for the rest of my life and wanted everybody to know that I was in it for the long haul.

The idea of "together forever" that both Jenny and Alia implicate is a recognizable love script. The women communicate a sense of certainty about the future of their relationship.

Even though Alia herself has experienced the end of a marriage, she does not hesitate to talk about marriage in terms of "forever" and "the long haul." Here she uses easily recognizable common discourse about love to show that her partnership with a man was somehow meant to be. Similarly, Jennifer states that after three weeks of knowing her current partner "we had pretty much decided we were gonna be together forever."

Chapter Two

Appearance

> I used to have a lot of women-symboled jewelry and lots of purple jewelry, most of it was jewelry stuff. I never, without those things, was assumed to be a lesbian at any point. And when I dated a very feminine woman, we dressed very very deliberately when we went out, so that it was clear that we were together. There were a couple of times that we didn't and we went to lesbian bars and we were made fun of for being heterosexuals who accidentally ended up in that environment. So, I dressed very very deliberately to appear lesbian. Jewelry choices, and lilies and women symbols and black triangles and that kinda thing. I also had a motorcycle jacket, you know, with all the zippers, that was purple and had gay symbols all over it. Pins, I put pins all over it. There is a particular fit of jeans that I used to wear that I would not be able to wear anymore, you know, boy jeans and big black belts and big chunky black shoes and I had very hip glasses that I wore, at least I thought that they were. It felt very dyky to me. (Jennifer)

The aesthetic of being a visible gay man or lesbian has been the concern of many scholarly works. A change in dress can sometimes accompany the process of coming out. Some lesbians, for example, report changing their physical appearance after coming out, by cutting their hair, wearing more masculine and/or casual clothes, no longer wearing makeup and shaving, and getting a tattoo or piercing (Krakauer and Rose 2002). But the processes involved in managing appearance after involvement with men is not necessarily the reverse of what happens when the women came out as lesbian, bisexual, or queer. Because so much is assumed from appearance, the women in some cases use their appearance to challenge assumptions about their identities. For some, dress becomes another way of telling a particular story about who they are.

Jennifer recounts how, when she was partnered with a woman, she deliberately worked to "appear" lesbian through her clothing and jewelry choices.

She and her partner did this consciously as a way of indicating membership in a particular cultural setting. Their claim to lesbian spaces and their right to be in those spaces were judged, she felt, on how well they performed "being a lesbian." In order to be lesbian, they had to "look" lesbian. Their identity claim was contingent on how well they visually projected the identity that they embraced.

The importance of one's appearance in interaction cannot be overstated. In part, people communicate who they are through their appearance, making clothing, hairstyles, and jewelry choice key elements in self-presentation (Gleeson and Frith 2003). Dress is a significant tool of identity performance, whether one is consciously or unconsciously utilizing it (Woodward 2005). Clothing, hairstyle, and jewelry are tools used by the wearer and they are read and interpreted by the viewer. Dress is a reflection of individual choices and preferences, but is also social in that it can serve as the basis for community belonging, or lack of belonging. It can be used to answer the question not just of who one is but where one belongs. There is an important connection here between gender and sexuality. When someone assumes they can guess another person's sexuality from their dress, they are generally relying on signs of gender non-conformity. Usually, a woman who is guessed to be lesbian is a woman who does not perform gender in conventional ways. Of course gender non-conformity does not always translate into identifying as non-heterosexual.

The accounts of the women with whom I spoke are as much about gender as they are about sexuality. The women in this study varied in the way they performed gender as lesbian, bisexual, and queer women. Some women found that partnership with a man affected the ways in which they performed their gender. For some, being with men gave them the opportunity to violate gender dress codes more readily. Because they were assumed to be heterosexual, the women allowed themselves to perform gender in a much less traditional way, at work, school, or in their homes, without fear of the effects of homophobia and gay bashing. Others expressed that their partnership with men actually allowed them to perform more of what they considered to be "themselves."

SEX/GENDER/DRESS/DESIRE

One's dress is always saturated with messages about one's gender and subsequently one's sexuality. Gender is constructed as a dichotomous system, composed of two "opposite" poles: male and female. Sexuality, a component of which is desire, is grounded in this system of two genders, where opposite attraction is labeled heterosexuality, same-gender attraction is homosexuality, and attraction to both genders is labeled bisexuality. Desire, like gender, is grounded in the dichotomous system. Dress is the primary tool for not only showcasing, but also inferring, or reading, someone's gender and by extension their sexuality. It can also serve as a tool for breaking the connection between gender and sexuality (Dozier 2005). Dress is potentially disruptive, as showcased, for example, by masculine lesbians managing the appearance of pregnancy (Ryan 2013).

DRESS AND LGBTQ IDENTITIES

In a society where it is sometimes risky or unsafe to disclose LGBTQ sexual identities, individuals use their appearance to communicate their belonging in various communities. Having embraced LGBTQ identities previously, the participants in this study are aware of the importance of appearance in negotiating identities, as the opening quotation from Jennifer indicates. Dress, including hair and accessories, plays an important role in communicating sexual desire and rendering the actor attractive to potential partners. In most social settings, LGBTQ identities are both marked and silenced. They are both regarded as deviant to a certain extent and also not given room for expression. In some settings, where openly disclosing an LGBTQ identity may have adverse consequences, one may utilize the body as a tool in order to render oneself visible (Gleeson and Frith 2003).

WHAT HAPPENS TO DRESS?

Although dress is an important part of navigating the change in partners for nearly all the women I interviewed, the way dress is negotiated varies. This does not necessarily translate into a change in appearance for all women. Some women do in fact change their appearance. Others navigate the change in partners by not changing anything about their appearance, thus showing that they are essentially the same person.

No Change

Interestingly, one of the women who reported no change in her dress was also one of the only two women who identified as straight after becoming involved with a man. When I asked Pam if she noticed any changes in her dress, she states: "No. I try to be as pretty for a girl as I try to be for a boy." Although Pam identifies as straight, she does not imply that she was somehow wrong in being attracted to women. Saying that she is "as pretty" when involved with women as she is with men implies that she is the "same person" despite the change in partners. By dressing in the same way before and after her involvement with men, Pam works to show that both decisions were extensions of her individual preference. In using the word "pretty," Pam also indicates that she has not in the past, nor is she now, trying to reject the normative standard of feminine beauty, again making the point that her dress is a reflection of her own aesthetic.

Karen also reported no change in her appearance. She states: "I was incredibly low-maintenance before and I'm incredibly low-maintenance now. Nothing changed." When I asked Karen about her attraction to men she states: "I've always been kinda comfortable with going to where my attraction takes me as long as it seems like it's healthy." For Karen, someone who is seeking to show that she is essentially the same person before and after her involvement with her male partner, saying that her appearance did not change helps maintain continuity between the past and the present. Karen is different from Pam, in that she does not emphasize embracing femininity.

I asked Nadia if anything about her appearance had changed. "No," she replied, "well, I mean, (laugh) fashions have changed." Like Karen and Pam, Nadia implied that she has made no conscious changes in her appearance. Any change is due to general changes in fashion trends. All three women identified as lesbian prior to their involvement with men. But their identity outcomes are all different. Karen now identifies as married,[1] Pam as heterosexual, and Nadia as bisexual. They nevertheless all use similar strategies to create a seamless identity trajectory, essentially saying, "I dress the same, therefore I am the same."

When I asked Mabel, a lesbian woman who now identifies as queer, if anything about her appearance had changed, she stated "Not really. The only thing that has changed are the pants that I wear." Subsequent to this fairly straightforward response, came a much more complicated and layered explanation of the changes in her appearance:

> [...] I always wear t-shirts and jeans. That's all I wear. But I used to wear boy-shorts all the time. [...] So, the only thing that's really changed about my appearances, through moving right now, I've packed up all my boy-shorts in the Good Will box and I'm gonna take all my boxes to the [local homeless shelter] and give them to homeless people. So, all my boy-shorts are in there. I don't wear those anymore. I wear girl-shorts. Like form fitting, I guess. Like these [pointing to the shorts she has on] are my favorite shorts. They're super comfortable and like, I don't look like a potato sack in them, which is what I looked like when I wore boy-shorts, but I suppose, lesbians are supposed to wear boy-shorts and be masculine looking, I guess is what I thought.

Mabel isolates her choice of shorts as the pivotal change in her appearance: boy-shorts versus girl-shorts. Boy-shorts make one look like a "potato sack" while girl-shorts are "form-fitting." But Mabel rescues her choice from being associated with conventional femininity, by stating that girl-shorts are comfortable. The point of giving away boy-shorts to charity is symbolically potent. When Mabel makes the point that she has given away her boy-shorts, she is essentially saying that her decision to be with men is permanent. This is something that no other interviewee communicated. It is true that Mabel could easily purchase more boy-shorts if she so chooses. But even if she does do so in the future, the power of sharing such a statement is not diminished.

Authentic Aesthetic

Some women indicated that nothing about their dress is different. But there were other women in the study who did not seek to establish sameness. Instead, they acknowledged that something in their dress had changed. But this change was not anchored in ideas of masculinity or femininity, as might be expected. The core of the issue of change had to do with visibility and heterosexual privilege.

Ayana indicated that something about her dress is different. The difference, however, was not about being any more or less feminine. Dress became less important in her identity performance. Her partnership with a man allowed Ayana the space to care less about the use of dress in managing her identity.

> I had to put so much care that my clothing reflected who I was and what I was feeling.... I'd probably be in the peasant shirt and whatever, but I can also go out of my house in jeans and T-shirts, and I don't have to work so hard to see what other people are born to perceive me as. I just don't have to care so much, I don't know.

Ayana explained that her claim to the lesbian identity could be challenged by virtue of her choice of dress. She assumed that she may not appear "legit" if she did not follow the guidelines for appropriate lesbian appearance. Ayana did not give any example of ways in which she had perhaps tried to appear more "legit." She simply stated that being partnered with a man affords her the opportunity to not even have to think about whether she would be read as having a claim on the identity that she embodied. Here, Ayana is balancing her personal identity and her social identity. She wishes for her dress to be a reflection of her own preferences, rather than a marker for a community with which she associates. By virtue of her partnership with a man, Ayana feels that her clothing can now solely reflect her choices, rather than her community affiliations. What Ayana is doing is not giving up the social part of dress, to replace it with the individual part of dress. She is in fact replacing one social aspect with another. She no longer aligns herself with the lesbian community. What she does instead, unwittingly, is align herself with heterosexuality, since heterosexuality is the default sexual category. Although she does not identify as such, she is read as straight. Margaret also recalled having felt a certain pressure to communicate the legitimacy of her claim to a lesbian identity through dress:

> When my ex-partner and I got together, she was like "do you see any differences between us?" And I'm like "yeah. You're a tomboy and I'm not. So what's the big deal?" I suspected that there are some issues there about, you know, if you identify in a certain way, how do you show up?

Margaret echoed the point that Ayana made about legitimacy. Both Margaret and Ayana assumed that the way in which they chose to dress influenced whether their claim was seen as legitimate. In both cases, the women saw themselves as not quite being able to fit into the standards. Abigail makes a similar point:

> I've never been super girly in my dress but as soon as I identified as bi, I wanted to look more butch because I perceived that there were people out there who were questioning whether I was really queer. Like I definitely remember getting dressed and being like "no, I think I'll wear these big baggy pants." I kinda felt like I had to put on a little show and play down my more feminine inclinations in order to look more sort of credibly queer.

She goes on to add:

> I remember being aware of it and I don't think like anyone else had said anything directly to me about it, but I just had that sense. And also it wasn't just about proving that I was really gay, but I was also being attractive to women. You know like feeling like wearing this thing is gonna make me more attractive to women.

Celia expresses similar sentiments:

> I've always been feminine, you know, like, I like clothes, shoes. I always have my make-up done. You know, was fussy about my appearance. I think unfortunately people still, I think it's changing, but I think people still have that stereotype that you've got to be butchy that you gotta be boyish and I still got attention from people but I don't think that they thought that I was a true lesbian. . . . Even before when I was dating a woman, people thought I was straight because I didn't look the part. People used to call me "the lipstick" and then, which drives me crazy, 'cause this is not 1950 but even when I was looking for women, I had a really hard time finding them because I don't think people thought I looked the part. People are still really big on the butch stereotype thing and even when I was in a club looking for somebody, I don't think that people thought that I was [lesbian]. I was always seen as straight.

All three indicate that regardless of how they chose to identify, part of being considered "really gay," "really queer," or a "true lesbian' is to have that performance accepted by others as authentic. Not performing their identities in ways that corresponded to the stereotypical notion of what a lesbian/queer person should look like threatened the women's claim to that identity. The highlighting of this threat is an important part of the storytelling process. By sharing the fact that they were considered by others to be not quite "real," the women open the door for the possibility of their involvement with men. None of the women denied that they were "really" attracted to other women and none, except the two women who identify as straight, denied their past experiences. But despite that fact, stating that they were considered by others to be inadequate performers allows them to then make room for their subsequent decisions. The pressure for Tina to perform her lesbian identity in a particular way was a bit different than what the other women shared.

> My girlfriend was always yammering at me about I wasn't femme enough, and I wasn't girly enough, and she was also very controlling so you know she didn't like the way I wore my hair unless I wore it a certain way. She didn't like the way I dressed unless I dressed a certain way. How in the world I got myself into that mess, I have no idea. But with my husband, you know, he's very, he actually likes the me that I like, so, I'm a lot more comfortable.

Because of the strict butch/femme division present in Tina's community, the pressure on her was to perform her lesbian identity in a more "girly" way than she was able to. Although the other women express having to be more butchy than they felt they were able to be, the dynamics here are similar. In terms of her appearance, Tina's quote also shows how she did not quite cut it. Jenny shared the following about her choice to dress in less feminine ways when involved with her female partner. Recall that Jenny is one of the women who now identifies as straight:

> I also took an introduction to feminism course and they were talking about the oppression of woman and how makeup is evil and bras are evil and stuff like that and so I was "oh man. We're being oppressed by this makeup crap" so as a rebellion to the whole male-dominance, I stopped looking like, I started looking like males, you know, funny enough. . . . I cut my hair short. I wouldn't wear makeup. I wore baggy pants, collared shirts. I thought that was what a lesbian was supposed to look like. Like I didn't know about lipstick lesbians back then, like *The L-Word*.

She continues to add that her appearance was one way that helped her mother find out about her relationship with another woman. But what Jenny shares here goes a bit beyond just a story about coming out to parents:

> My mom found out. . . . I mean I changed my whole look. You know, I cut my hair short. I stopped wearing make-up. I looked like a construction worker,

like dressed like that or what not. Very very got into it. So obviously she knew something was up.

Jenny counted her decision to cut her hair and stop wearing makeup as elements of her decision to get into her role as a lesbian. The phrase "got into it" gives Jenny the ability to create some distance between herself and her previous identity. By saying that she "got into it," Jenny is perhaps establishing her previous performance as something that did not truly come from within her. She recognized that commonly acceptable markers for a lesbian identity existed and she stated that she used those markers, but she inferred that she did not really feel like that was an authentic identity for her. Appearance was a recurring theme in Jenny's interview. She shared a conversation she had with her father about the lesbian look:

> Like one day, this is all before my mom found out, so he tells me "so do you know what a lesbian would look like?" and I'm like "what do you mean?" I knew exactly what he was getting at because he meant me, like he wanted me to describe me . . . and I adamantly denied that you could tell if somebody was gay just by the way they dress and even if that's partly not true but I completely denied that. I mean he had to have known.

Jenny indicated that in order to not come out to her father, she denied that one's dress is a marker for one's sexual identity. In the tone of the description of that incident, it becomes clear that Jenny herself very much believed that one can predict sexuality by appearance. The "right" to look however she wants is something she associated with her current relationship. She indicated that she can be both more masculine and more feminine in her current relationship. In her previous relationship, Jenny said that she looked like a construction worker. She also used the term "butch" to describe herself. The description of her appearance before, and her use of the phrase "got into it," gives one the impression that she saw herself as performing for some audience, something that she does not associate with her current identity. Interestingly, Jenny recalled that her male partner thought short hair was "cute" and convinced her to cut her hair short once again after they became involved.

Male Partners

The way the women performed their lesbian, bisexual, and queer identities prior to their involvement with men is varied. The way they signal the shift is varied, and the way they present themselves once partnered with men is also varied. Abigail and Tina were keenly aware of the heterosexualizing nature of their relationships. They explained how the presence, whether implied or actual, of their male partners made partaking in gender non-conformist dress less problematic.

> It's funny, I think I actually looked more like lesbian, after I started dating my husband because I cut my hair really short. (Abigail)

Tina talks about how she performs her gender after involvement with men:

> Oddly enough, it is so much easier not trying to be that that femme. . . . I'm probably a lot more butch and he allows me to be more aggressive than [my ex] allowed me to be and in a weird way, I think I'm actually probably just more butch now than I was in the lesbian relationship, but again, I mean, as long as you got that ring on your finger and a husband to pull out, in this town, it's alright.

With a male partner, their gender non-conformity is not likely to be read as equivalent to a lesbian identity. Several different dynamics are at play, allowing the women to claim that they were dressing more like themselves. They were in relationships and assumed to be heterosexual. But the protection of their heterosexual relationship also allowed the women room to explore non-traditional gender performances without fear of homophobia, because of the assumption that the women are heterosexual. In this case, the women indicated that they would push the boundaries of conventional gender attire, but their relationships with men made it so the potential threat of this violation was diminished. So, it is less risky for these women to publically challenge normative gendered dress, because their challenges are couched in implied heterosexuality. Because of this overwhelming assumption of heterosexuality, even deliberate efforts to challenge normative gender dress is often less than effective. Heather expressed her concern about the invisibility associated with being partnered with a man:

> Like I thought about trying to do something with my hair or clothing that reads more androgynous, or more counter-cultural, so that, if somebody sees me kissing him, it's a shock. It's a jolt and they'd have to think about it. And it's not like I need to make my entire personal life a political act for somebody else's edification or something. It's just that I feel like stagnated and invisible.

Her partnership with her male partner rendered Heather invisible. She was no longer "marked." Heather worked to restigmatize her body in order to maintain some sort of claim on her previous identity. This is done more or less effectively, depending in part on the physical presence and appearance of her male partners. A man who is attracted to a woman in violation of appropriate gender dress rules, may be said to be a man not like other men. As mentioned in the previous chapter, invoking an image of a man who is different from others is useful for creating a seamless self-narrative. The presence of a man brings about the assumption of heterosexuality. But the way that the women and their partners perform their gender is also important in how the relationship is read. Not every woman who is with a man is unproblematically recognized as straight. Chloe remembers an incident when she was at a festival with her male partner:

> We were holding hands and I specifically remember like this older man, and he cocked his head and he was looking at us, like "huh." I don't know that we were really taken as a cliché heterosexual couple.

It is not possible, nor should it be the goal, to document what this older man was actually reacting to. This quote is significant because Chloe used it as a way to highlight the power of her own gender non-conformity. Chloe describes herself as "not feminine enough" and remembers feeling "pretty dykish with my boyfriend." The fact that she was in a public space with a male partner did not necessarily feminize her androgynous look. Similarly, Riley explained that she embodies a "female masculinity" and describes her style as that of a "14-year-old boy." She explained that she is probably not mistaken for heterosexual even in the company of her male partners. She assumed that people recognize that:

> There's something slightly off at least sort of gender-wise, because if you get down to it, you know, I am aggressive and I don't shave my legs and a lot of times I have short hair and I drive a big station wagon and it's a five speed. You know I have these markers but then I'm sleeping with him. If it ever goes past that, I think "what is it about me as a dude that makes you like me?"

As Riley and Chloe's comments show, for women who perform a nontraditional femininity, the presence of a man is not always enough to mainstream their performance. If anything, the women's performance can sometimes have implications for how the male partner's gender and sexuality is read. Chloe mentioned an instance where her male partner tried to change her appearance by buying her a dress and encouraging her to grow out her hair. I can't make assumptions about what Chloe's partner's intentions were in trying to get her to appear more traditionally feminine, but the point here is that far from being read as traditionally heterosexual, Chloe assumed that her partner's gender and/or sexuality was being (re)defined by virtue of his involvement with her.

Beth states that she had always been surprised at the idea that a man would be attracted to her because of her appearance. In Beth's case, her outward appearance not only redefined the nature of the relationship with her male partner but it also colored assumptions about her male partner's gender and sexuality.

I'd be like "my boyfriend whatever," and people were like "when did he start to transition?" because they read me as so gay with my no hair, and then I'd have to go into like, "never (sigh), he's a bio-boy, you know, he can't help it." ... People that I met without him around, like queer people, like new queer people, would still read me as queer. And usually someone would tell them that I had a partner that was a bio-boy, like it would come up somehow or another and like they'd be like "really?" and there were people who were like "really, you know that you're gay, right?"

Because of Beth's outward appearance, people in interactions with her assumed that her partner was transgender, as opposed to assuming that Beth was heterosexual. This is the point that Hope clearly articulates:

How people see me depends on how I choose to visually present myself that day. If I'm wearing a dress or a skirt or something like that, people kind of see my hair [which is short] and they'll see who I'm with but they'll adjust. They'll adjust their view for that but if I'm looking more masculine or whatever, they adjust for that too and then also for the person I'm with.

The women's gender performance is not isolated from assumptions about their sexuality, and their partner's gender and sexuality. Perceptions of masculinity and femininity are mediating factors in what assumptions are made about the sexual identity of the women before and after their involvement with men.

The way each woman uses dress to navigate the change to a partner of a different gender is dependent on what kind of story she wishes to tell about herself. These women tell stories of continuation, regardless of their identities prior to becoming involved with men. They seek to be read as the "same person." In order to be read as the same person, some indicate that they dress in the same way that they used to. In this case, they use dress as a way to tell a story of self that is continuous. The same self that was involved with women is now involved with men. But this is only part of the dress story. The women also have to manage how they are being viewed by others and what their dress says about them. This is where the ways of navigating dress is further differentiated between the women. There are some women, like Ayana, who seem to be at ease with being themselves without having to acknowledge community belonging. She explains the change in her dress as anchored in the pressure she felt to look "lesbian." If there is a change in her dress, Ayana argues, it is because she can now show her real self: before, her real self was hidden. What Ayana is not accounting for is that, by not deliberately aligning herself with a non-straight community (whether it be bisexual, lesbian, or queer), and by virtue of the presence of her male partners, she will often be read as straight. She presents a narrative in which she feels that the only decision she is making is to either dress how she wants to or dress in line with some community standard, but then she is not the only one determining how she will be perceived. The social part of the navigation of dress includes how it is perceived by others. Unwittingly, Ayana is in fact aligned with a community. It is the more amorphous heterosexual community. And so, although Ayana indicates that she is not identifying as heterosexual by virtue of being involved with a man, she is nevertheless read as such. For Ayana, this is not a problem.

For women, like Heather, for whom this is a problem, a way has to be found to continue to signal a non-straight identity strongly enough to combat the assumption of heterosexuality. But even this process is complicated. As Tina explains, as long as one is partnered with a man, in a way that is publicly recognized or visible, dress that signals resistance to the standards of feminine beauty is somehow forgiven. For someone like Heather, the task is to challenge the appropriate display of gender enough to make the partnership with a man seem problematic. That is, the goal is to be so disruptive in dress that not only does the partnership with a male partner not forgive the transgression, but in fact, the transgression casts doubt on the nature of the partnership, or the sexual identity of the individuals involved, including the male partner. Women, like Heather, who wish to engage in such a level of disruption find themselves pitted against the heterosexual regime that imputes a heterosexual identity on everyone unless otherwise challenged. These women's success at posing a sufficient enough challenge by virtue of dress alone is further complicated by the physical presence or absence of their male partners. Thus, using dress to challenge heterosexuality and indeed heteronormativity meets with varying levels of success.

Cases where the women's dress is used by themselves to express their identity, or in cases where they perceive their dress is used by others to impute an identity on them, are both instances where the individual and social nature of dress have come into play. Dress carries not only the meanings that the wearer chooses to attach to it, but it also carries the observer's perceptions, communal symbols, and the cultural meanings attached to it.

NOTE

1. Married is not usually considered a sexual identity. But Karen uses it as such. It is perhaps in a way a tactic to imply that anything prior to the status of married is irrelevant.

Chapter Three

Not Bisexual

People don't like bisexual people and I didn't want to be one. (Jennifer)

The study of bisexuality is uniquely positioned to show underlying assumptions about sexuality as a whole. As an identity in the "sexual borderlands" (Callis 2014), not heterosexual or homosexual, bisexuality is a useful way to gauge the women's engagement with a variety of concepts concerning sexual identification.

When I tell people what my research is about, most like to venture a guess that women who were once partnered with women and now with men think of themselves as bisexual. This, in fact, is not totally accurate. Whether they choose to embrace the label, to dismiss it outright, or to theoretically engage it, bisexuality is an ever-present concept in their narratives.

PERCEPTIONS

Bisexuality seems to still exist at the margin of the margin, that is excluded from both heterosexual and gay and lesbian communities (Ochs and Rowley 2009). Numerous people identify as bisexual but their lives are not at the heart of research or public discussion about sexuality. Lack of knowledge about bisexual lives is supplemented by negative media images (Capulet, 2010). The women in this study are aware of negative perceptions of bisexual people. Bisexuality implies attraction to both genders, but each gender is considered the "opposite" of the other. It also implies a combination of two opposite orientations, namely, hetero- and homosexual. In essence, bisexuals make things complicated.

Because the women in this study are so often thought to be bisexual and because of bisexuality's interesting and ambiguous position in the system of sexual classification, there is much to be learned about how the women understand their own identities after their involvement with men.

At a glance, it may seem that identifying as bisexual is the most attractive identity outcome for women in this study. Thirteen women, out of the 32 interviewed, identified as bisexual after their involvement with men. And yet, stating that nearly a third of the women are now bisexual would be misleading. Although many women responded "bisexual" to the question about their current sexual identity, it soon became clear that the label is in many cases not adequate.

Jennifer's concise statement sums up the feeling that what other people feel about bisexuals, of course, informs whether the women would want to be considered bisexual. This is the only instance where one of the women actually articulates that she did not choose the label of bisexual precisely because of the stigma attached to it. But even though others did not express the same sentiment this succinctly, it is not unreasonable to think that it can in part explain why the women would be so hesitant to be called bisexual. Below, I will examine three key themes that emerge as the women engage the notion of bisexuality, namely, sex/gender/sexuality, authenticity, and essentialism and identity.

SEX, GENDER, AND SEXUALITY

The women in this study have experienced a change to a partner of a different gender and they struggle to understand what this change means for their own sexual identity. Through their thoughts about bisexuality, the women make clear that they see the inextricable way that sex, gender, and sexuality are connected. This connection makes it so questions regarding their own sexual identity are an inevitable consequence of the change to a partner of a different gender.

By virtue of being attracted to individuals of either gender, bisexuality questions the very assumption that genders are opposites. Similarly, bisexuality by functioning as a combination of heterosexual and homosexual experiences (including behavior and attraction) challenges the assumption that the two identities are opposites and that there are only two legitimate choices. The women in this study certainly see that there is a strong connection between the dichotomous organization of gender and that of sexuality. The women are unconvinced that bisexuality has the power to sufficiently challenge those systems.

For Heather, who now identifies as queer after having identified as lesbian, the term bisexual reinforces gender categories:

> It's still about packaging people in little boxes so that they're identifiable. This person is male. This person is female. This person is heterosexual. This person

is homosexual. And bisexual sort of challenges that but in a way, it doesn't, because bisexuals generally are viewed as one gender or the other, being attracted to two different genders. So it stays within that gender slash biological sex binary that keeps those boundaries.

Heather explains that bisexuality actually does little to disrupt the dichotomous nature of gender since bisexual attraction is generally understood as attraction to individuals of either or both genders. The category of bisexuality locates itself within the current system of sexual classification and does little to challenge the categories. For Heather, this is an unappealing aspect of bisexuality. Notice that Heather hopes that bisexuality does in some way disrupt gender but she then makes the statement that perhaps it does not in fact have the power to do that. What Heather values is a more fluid notion of gender and sexuality.

Celia makes a similar connection between the rigidity of sexual categories and the rigidity of gender categories. Speaking about being labeled bisexual, she states:

> And, I just really feel the need to say that that's not, that's not me, you're not understanding, I don't even like being categorized as bisexual. I don't like categories. I just want to be who I am. These are the things that I'm attracted to in people in general in whatever body they, that comes in, you know, is the body that it comes in. So I kinda take that on as my mission to educate the people around me that you know, you don't need to be so rigid in seeing people in terms of male and female.

Celia argues that sexuality doesn't have to be organized around gender at all. She brings up the person discourse to explain her attraction, meaning that she is attracted to a person regardless of their gender. Her understanding is that the current system of sexual classification is too narrowly based on bodies, or biological sex. Celia's resistance to the label of bisexual shows that for her, the term does not necessarily have the emancipatory quality that some have argued it does. Bisexual implies for her an attraction to people of either gender and Celia would like to make it clear that her attraction is actually not based on gender, or sex, at all.

Speaking about taking on a bisexual label, Emily states:

> I also don't think that I value the label, 'cause to me the label is "I'm committed to someone right now." It doesn't matter that it's a man or a woman, which, I hate saying that because I actually feel like it does something unhelpful to people, you know, that they choose to be in relationships with just men or just women and that is vitally important. So, I feel like saying things like "it's just not important" weakens, I mean, it is important, for someone, and I don't know if I'm making sense on this.

Emily argues that her relationship status is more salient to her than the gender of her partner. She also, like Celia, used the person discourse to explain her attraction. By trying to argue that gender is not the hallmark of how she organizes sexuality, Emily realizes that she can be seen as doing a disservice to gay and lesbian communities that are chiefly organized around the gender of the object of attraction. Emily recognizes this and hopes that her desire to reject gender as the organizing basis of her attractions doesn't do harm or "weaken" the gay and lesbian political claim. She says "I hate saying that because I actually feel like it does something unhelpful to people." Emily makes visible the clearest connection between identity and community. She realizes that the gendered organization of sexuality has led to the establishment of political communities. It seems that even if she was able to, Emily would not want to disrupt that organization. Emily is caught between how she would like to label her desire and what she sees as the basis for community organization. The struggle between what feels right individually and what feels right for a community will be explored further in a later chapter.

By calling on the "person" discourse, Celia and Emily seem to also be expressing their resistance to the idea that their own identities need to change based on the fact that they now find themselves in partnerships with men. When they stress that they are attracted to the person, both women imply that the current system of sexual classification is forcing them to confess some change within themselves where no change has taken place. The term *bisexual*, which could potentially offer the women a sense of continuity, actually does not seem to be a good fit because, as they explain it, bisexuality still implies a compartmentalization of desire or attraction. The term for them still implies that there is something fundamentally different about being attracted and involved with a woman as opposed to a man. Like Celia and Emily, Juliana explains that bisexual is an inadequate label for her:

> I mean partially because the connotation that there's two, you know, only two sexes and partially because, I don't know, I just don't like a label. I just don't, you know like there's some times when I feel like, there's some weeks where I feel more attracted to women. There's more, there's some weeks when I'm more attracted to men, or there's some weeks where I feel like I'm asexual. It's, if you wanna have a label. Whatever, and I just don't, whatever, you know I don't want, even myself, you know, but, I don't know, 'cause, I just feel like it changes, you know, I just feel like it changes, you know. So, I guess that term is kinda limiting.

Juliana's main concern with the inadequacy of the bisexual label is that it limits attraction to two genders. She thinks of bisexuality as implying equal, continuous, or simultaneous attraction to both men and women. She then explains that her attraction to men and women is neither continuous nor simultaneous. Again, Juliana is unable to find use for the label of bisexual and instead finds herself limited by it.

Through their engagement with the label of bisexual, the women communicate that they see a connection between systems of gender and sexual categorization. They are at times bothered by this connection and generally frustrated with the fact that individuals should be classified according to their gender and sexuality. They don't see bisexuality as a way to disrupt those systems.

AUTHENTICITY

> I'm bisexual . . . [that] just is a very loaded word and anybody who has identified as that knows that it comes associated with flakiness and indecisiveness and all these derogatory things. (Karen)

As Karen mentions, bisexual is a loaded word. Many women in this study make references to how bisexuals are generally perceived. More specifically, the women are particularly concerned with how bisexuals are perceived by lesbians. The lesbian perception of bisexuals and the relationship between lesbian and bisexual women has been the subject of much scholarship. It has been shown that for many reasons lesbians express a mistrust of bisexual women (Israel and Mohr 2004). One of the reasons is the uncertainly about bisexual women's political allegiances, mentioned earlier. The women in this study are aware of these perceptions. They find themselves negotiating these perceptions as they make sense of their own identities. Of all the baggage that comes with the label of bisexual, it seems that the lack of authenticity is the main underlying thread. According to the women in this study, bisexuality lacks authenticity. The reason why they believe this illuminates what they consider to be an authentic identity in the first place.

Margaret, who came out in the 1980s, remembers the earlier perceptions of bisexuals:

> It was no B in the GLBT . . . I really struggled, especially when bisexuality had just, you know, somebody might as well just call you a slut, right out.

Margaret is right in stating that there was no B in GLBT. The 1980s were a particularly difficult time for bisexual individuals. Bisexuals were generally thought to have caused the AIDS crisis, by serving as a bridge between the "gay disease" and straight society. Many gay and lesbian organizations were adamant about their refusal to include bisexual individuals in their membership (Rust 2001). Bisexuals have since became part of, and yet apart from, the gay and lesbian community.

The idea that bisexuals are not to be counted on politically or cannot be political allies because they have the option to identify as straight if they so choose is a common misperception. It implies that bisexuals make a choice with regard to their sexuality where no choice really can be made, the assumption being that sexuality is something that one is born into. Anyone who makes a "choice" or who has a choice is thus expressing an inauthentic self. Choice implies inauthenticity. Anne touches precisely on this idea of inauthenticity:

> [T]here's this strong belief among the lesbian culture that, or my experience, that . . . if you're bisexual, you're really just experimenting.

If one is experimenting, one cannot potentially be counted on as a political ally. The argument is that real sexuality is not fluid. Bisexuals are not considered to have authentic identities because bisexuality is not considered stable. The idea that bisexuals are "just experimenting" is a theme that emerges time and time again in the women's accounts. Although the women may not themselves identify as bisexual, by virtue of having been involved with women and now with men, they still have to contend with some of the stereotypes that accompany the label of bisexual.

Amy echoes Anne's point that the lesbian perception of bisexuals is that they are experimenting or somehow in transition:

> I know another bisexual woman who said that her girlfriend was often complaining about bisexual women, you know, that they didn't mean it.

The point is that attraction to women is something that one has to "mean," implying that it is something that should consistently be the basis of identity. A change in partners is seen as indecisiveness, as an example of not having "meant it." Another issue is, of course, that of non-monogamy. Non-monogamy is commonly associated with bisexuality. For these women, non-monogamy has to be rejected in order to allow them to present a stable sense of themselves. Again the connection between stability and authenticity is established. Nala also touches on the notion of stability:

> The stereotype [is] that people that are bisexual are promiscuous, that they are greedy, that, maybe people won't take me seriously, that, oh it's just a phase.

Nala believes that the label would make others not take her seriously since bisexuality is regarded as a phase, as experimenting as Anne called it. Phases and experiments need not be taken seriously because they lack stability and thus authenticity. Abigail addresses a broader perception of bisexuals:

> I feel like there was always this sort of under-current in the gay community at school and in the broader culture, as well, like you know, like reading queer studies stuff or even like, Out magazine or something. Just that bi people aren't really queer, or aren't really gay, the queer part of it isn't real.

Abigail's perception is that bisexual people are not really viewed as part of the queer community. Abigail used the term queer, not as a gender-disrupting concept, but as a cumulative term, referring to both gays and lesbians. Abigail also mentions notions of authenticity. "The queer part of it isn't real" expresses precisely this idea that if bisexuality is made of both heterosexuality and homosexuality, that the homosexual part is inauthentic. She is able to tease out many of the stereotypes that are often associated with bisexuals.

> That [bisexuals] should just, you know, buck up and choose. [...] I think that often people think that you can't make a choice or my personal favorite and when I say favorite I mean least favorite is that you're experimenting. [...] Like this isn't your real life. Eventually, you know you'll start, you know you'll make your choice and that'll be it. (Abigail)

Abigail echoes some of the elements that Anne brought up earlier, including the fact that bisexuals are not sincere in their desires, that they are just experimenting, and that they are failing to make a choice. Notice again the mention of one's "real life." Abigail reiterates that her experience is read as inauthentic or not real. Celia recalls that lesbians around her had what she perceived as fear of abandonment:

> I guess fear, about taking a relationship to the next level because they were always worried that I was really straight and was gonna go back to a man, or that I was afraid to give up what they would call heterosexual privilege and that I was gonna leave them. [...] Little jokes would always be "oh yes, the bisexual girlfriend" you know or "when is she gonna go back to, you know, her real life." Or "when is she going to finally realize that she's a dyke. She needs to come out." You know, it was just, never truly feeling like I was accepted. So, this was from girlfriends and from you know, say, people in the community or the bar scene. [...]

What Celia recalled is that her bisexual identity is thought to be transitional. She implies that the women around her were merely waiting for her to settle into either "real" identity, "dyke" or "heterosexual." Heather engages the notion of authenticity more directly:

> There's this sense people have that you're supposed to pick. You have to pick a camp and you have to stay in your camp. And if you haven't picked, then you're being dishonest, or you haven't dealt with something, or you're trying to have the best of both worlds, or bla bla bla ... which I feel like is crap but I

don't want to watch that go through people's minds or listen to it come out of their mouths.

Heather brings up again the notion of stability. What is necessary for identities to be considered authentic is stability, or staying in one's camp. It is "dishonest" or perhaps even misleading or deceitful not to make a choice that neatly falls within the established categories. Hope makes a similar point, stating that bisexuality is seen as a developmental step between a straight and lesbian identity:

> Bisexuality is really held at arm's length. I mean it's one of those places where I think a lot of people believe it doesn't exist. That it's not a real place to be. No one had produced bisexual theory. I think people are just starting to. [...] people say, you know, bisexuality for a woman is just a step before being a lesbian when she can't totally admit that she only likes women or that she still has, you know, internalized homophobia.

Because it is considered a step between two real identities, straight and lesbian, bisexuality is in itself not considered real, not authentic. It is considered at best, a mid-point. Mabel mentions the same concerns that many other women have, that bisexuals are seen as greedy and indecisive:

> I mean there's some issues in the gay community with lesbians and gay men who don't like bisexuals. There's some problems with that in the community because they think [bisexuals] need to pick a side and they're greedy or whatever they want to say about it. And, personally I've never had anything against people who call themselves bisexual unless they're only calling themselves bisexual because they're questioning their sexuality. That bothers me. If they're questioning their sexuality they need to say that they're questioning their sexuality and not give themselves a label because to me that undermines somebody who truly is bisexual. So, I guess, I've moved on, down the label of gay stuff, where once, I was just a lesbian and now I'm queer. I mean, I'm still in that community and I guess I have a different point of view from it now.

What is rather unique about Mabel's take on bisexuality is that it is very important for her to separate people whom she considers "truly bisexual" from those whom she considers "questioning." Mabel seems to believe that people who are "questioning," who are making up their minds, will hurt bisexual individuals who have made up their mind and happen to have settled on bisexuality. Mabel engages the notion of authenticity but unlike other women, she actually believes that there is a way to do bisexuality authentically and by contrast a way to do it inauthentically. She is the only person who makes this distinction. Mabel, however, does not herself identify as bisexual. She chooses to identify as queer.

By examining the women's perception of the label of bisexual, it becomes clear that the women value the notion of an authentic identity. A change in partners challenges notions of stability and thus threatened authenticity.

ESSENTIALISM AND IDENTITY

As the women work to disentangle notions of stability and authenticity, another strong theme emerges. The chief complaint of women about the label of bisexual is that it "doesn't fit" them. A couple of questions come up. What exactly does it not fit? And why should it fit? In the following accounts, the women grapple with this notion of labels and fit. Through this discussion, it becomes clear that many women view sexual identity as something that precedes language. In her analysis of bisexuality, Jennifer Baumgartner states "sexuality is not who you sleep with, it's who you are. It doesn't change according to who is standing next to you" (2007:6). For Baumgarter, sexual behavior (who you sleep with) and relationship status (who is standing next to you) are roughly the same in importance. And it seems that the women in this study would agree with Baumgarter. Although they stop short of asserting that one is born with a particular sexual identity, what could be considered classic essentialism, they do hint at the notion of having an identity that is real akin to the notion of a "true self." Riley states:

> I always avoided identifying completely and if I sort of, forced to, I would say I'm queer. But, I've always had a big aversion to saying bisexual because I felt like it was just too sort of . . ., claiming an identity for me has always been sort of problematic because I felt like it was not giving me space. It was sort of targeting me. . . . I'm always incredibly worried that someone is going to call me bisexual, like I just, out of all these sort of stations that people can be put in, I abhor that place the most . . . I would say straight before I would say bisexual 'cause it's just like, partially because of the stigma I've given it and this sort of, the binary quality of it and the social stigma around it. I don't want to be part of this group that is like . . ., like Lindsay Lohan is in a relationship with a woman now, or there's that song "I kissed a girl and I liked it," like I don't want to be that, you know what I see it as and larger society sees it as, as this hip thing, 'cause it further, sort of, delegitimizes the experience, I feel like. And it's such a term, like as opposed to maybe lesbian or gay, although those are terms that have come from outside and have turned in, I feel like it's even more so created by majority society, just sort of, let's label this anomaly. You know there's all these jokes, on both sides, like "Isn't that just a town on the trip to gay-town."

I quote Riley at length here because she explores many important themes about bisexuality. Riley believes that labels in general, and the bisexual label in particular, are limiting and not giving her "space." The idea that one's identity needs more "space" than a given label can provide is unintentionally essentialist. Riley is making the assumption that her identity precedes the label that she will use to describe it. She believes that she has a self, a true self, that is not entirely reflected in the language that is at her disposal. Many women who spoke of the inadequacy of labels seem to have a similar complaint. Labels, they explain, do not capture the entirety of their self. The notion that a real sexual self resides within the individual is a belief not limited to the women in this study. It can be argued in fact that common knowledge about sexual identity relegates it to a place within the individual.

Riley explains that she "abhors" being taken for bisexual more than she would "straight." Although she is disturbed by the "lack of space" under the label of bisexual, she would still prefer the lack of space under the label of straight.

For Riley, bisexual comes with "stigma." She makes several references to media representations of bisexuality, including the actor Lindsay Lohan, who recently had a much-publicized relationship with another female celebrity, and the popular song by Katy Perry about having a brief encounter with a girl. For Riley, these media representations of bisexuality reinforce the stereotype that bisexual individuals are not serious in their commitments to their same-gender partners, making bisexuality a fad or a "hip" trend.

Riley also seems to believe that the term "bisexual" is different from gay or lesbian. She believes that the term has somehow been imposed from the "outside" in order to categorize an "anomaly." In a seemingly unrelated note, she goes back to the theme of impermanence. By repeating a joke, Riley brings up the fact that bisexuality is sometimes thought of "on both sides"—meaning from both gay/lesbian and straight communities—as a developmental step between straight and gay, a step that some people will move through as they seek to come out. For these reasons, Riley would rather be anything but bisexual. In her engagement with the label of bisexual, notions of authenticity or lack of authenticity are also visible. In her account, pop-culture, celebrities and music are all examples of fleeting and inauthentic commodities. Riley expresses her desire to be aligned with something more real that reflects her true self.

The women in the study recognize that no label, at least none that they currently know of, is the perfect fit. They do not seem hopeful that such a label even exists. What they do acknowledge is that their engagement with the system of sexual categorization will always be less than perfect. Although the women often expressed that they were not satisfied with the language available to them to translate their sexual selves, they nevertheless settled on some available label, in some cases, on the label bisexual. It seems, although labels are imperfect, they are needed. Jill makes this point very clearly:

> I find like the whole labeling system problematic. And have for some time, but I also feel like it's what we have. I don't really like the labels either, you know, but I feel like it's important to still engage them and challenge that, you know, because I feel like the label lesbian, yes it's problematic, but it's there and we can't ignore it. Just because it's problematic, just because it's constricted, just because the boundaries are really squishy doesn't make it less real.

Identities translate into communities. Many women express a desire to live without labels but many of those same women have words to describe themselves, whether it be bisexual, queer, or straight. Although they feel that labels are problematic, in many ways, they have recognized that it is nearly impossible to navigate interaction with others without a label. Recall Emily's point about communities:

> It doesn't matter that it's a man or a woman, which, I hate saying that because I actually feel like it does something unhelpful to people, you know, that they choose to be in relationships with just men or just women and that is vitally important. So, I feel like saying things like "it's just not important" weakens, I mean, it is important, for someone.

Emily is aware that there is power in claiming labels. Communities are built on particular identities. The women make an important connection between label and identity and their power to create communities and in some cases motivate political action. Hope sheds light on why one might use the label although it feels inadequate:

> I usually don't identify, I kind of like to, not shy away from that, but I think people kind of put you in categories very easily. Bisexual is something that most people understand really well. I don't necessarily, it's not my favorite term, I think it's still really, it denotes a separation of gender, and I kind of, I think there's more of a middle point.

Hope uses the label because it makes sense to people with whom she interacts. Here Hope brings up an important point. Individuals need language to communicate their desires and selves to others. Although living without a label would be ideal, Hope finds that it is necessary to label herself in order to make herself understood.

Pennie was one of those participants who self-identified as bisexual at the beginning of the interview. But the quote that follows presents some of her thought processes as she chose to settle on that label. What becomes evident is that Pennie didn't choose the label because she feels that it reflects who she is as a person.

> It's something I'm constantly saying to people like you don't have to be either straight or lesbian, you know, there is a space between, whether you want to

> call it bisexual or polyamorous or whatever you want to label it as. So that has always been a discussion that I've had with people about that. I mean I label myself as bisexual but really it's a term that I use but I don't think it really fits me. I like pretty much a person for whoever they are, doesn't matter what parts they come with or how they perform their gender. I use bisexual usually to avoid getting into all of the, like a discussion of all of that. Like if I feel like I can't have that discussion with that person, like if I feel like they won't really understand what's going on, sometimes I'll just choose to just say I'm bisexual.

Although initially Pennie indicates that she is bisexual, after further discussion, it becomes clear that she is not necessarily committed to that label. She chooses to label herself as bisexual because it is familiar to people. The reason why she feels that the label does not fit her is because she considers her attraction as one that disregards gender rather than as a preference for individuals of either gender. She understands bisexual as something in between gay and straight and a label that reinforces the dichotomous gender division. The bisexual label is for her not a reflection of her true self but a way to create a standpoint from which to speak, albeit temporarily. Margaret seems outright offended by the fact that the label bisexual obscures the variety of experience and attractions that she feels. She is "insulted" she says at the "simplification."

> I think that they were devaluing, you know, kinda, like there's so much, there's so much to what you enjoy as a person, so much to how you experience your life and I feel like to kind of boil it down into a multiple choice is just, it's such a simplification, it's almost insulting. […] I don't know, I feel like my preference is to not have a label at all. […] I just accept myself for what I am, more than ever, who I am is just, who I am is not who I'm attracted to. Just not. It's like one small part of me. Completely. I think that's why I don't have a—the whole label thing—you know, it doesn't really concern me that much. […] Maybe I want to label but I don't know. I guess, I don't know. I guess I'm bisexual. That's, that's, I don't, I don't introduce myself as, hardly as that though, you know.

Margaret explains that who she is, is more than who she is attracted to, attraction in fact is a small part of who she is. Labels, she explains, are for those for whom attraction is a larger part of who they are, although she does not indicate who those people may be. What is most interesting is despite the initial outrage, Margaret still closes her statement by declaring herself bisexual. Labels, it seems, are inescapable. Juliana has a similar engagement with the label of bisexual:

> I would see myself as fluid in identity as far as not being particularly, you know, I don't feel like I'm bisexual but I feel, sometimes I say that to people in order to make a quick response to them in who I like. But, I really don't like

that term and, because you know, I, I feel like I can have the ability to fall in love with whoever, you know.

Juliana feels that she can "fall in love with whoever," meaning that gender does not necessarily limit how she chooses partners. Bisexual, for her, implies attention to gender. It implies attraction to people of both genders. And that is limiting to her. Despite the fact that the label of bisexual doesn't fit her experience in many ways, Juliana chose to adopt the label in order to facilitate communication with others.

When the women share that they find labels inadequate or inaccurate or limiting, they lay the groundwork for the possibility that they will be using creative methods to translate their experience into language. Individuals need to make themselves understood to others and below Nala acknowledges that point:

I just hate labels in general, right, because, like I said at the very beginning, like I used to self-identify as white and half of me, like half of my upbringing is really is white, but half of it, is Greek. Right, like my father's an immigrant, but there's, there's no label for that in like the check box on the census. Like, there's nothing for that and, I don't know. Yeah, I don't know. I don't know. I don't know what to call myself. I think academia is really convoluted my sense of words. There's not a label that I think I'm really comfortable with, right, because I could call myself like omni-sexual or what's the other one, there is, there's another one that, but it's just that—
Poly-sexual?
Right. Right. But no one uses those words. No one outside of like women and gender studies departments use those words so it's like, it's not really useful.

Nala explains the taken-for-granted notion that people's identities need to make sense to others. Nala is not free to express herself in any capacity that she chooses because after all, she needs to make herself understood to others.

Choosing a label provides the opportunity to claim authenticity. But this is perhaps the same reason why the label of bisexual is of little use to these women. The label itself lacks authenticity. So although it seems like it would "fit" the experience of women who have both partnered with men and with women, these women need labels, as others do, that give their experience authenticity. The label of bisexual fails to deliver on this front. Other labels don't necessary deliver fully on this front either. Thus the women find themselves moving in and out of labels and carving out authenticity through the strategic use of labels as opposed to accepting them without condition. There is just so much power one has, as an individual, to portray and maintain an accurate picture of themselves. To be read as bisexual forces these women to contend with the perceptions of bisexuality even if they fail to identify as such. By no means does this imply that bisexuality is useless as an identity or as a label. Labels have different purposes for different people and sometimes even for the same people. Individuals need a way to anchor themselves in the sexuality discourse. Bisexuality works as a temporary place marker for some women. Although it fails to bring about all the disruption that some have argued it can bring, it works in some situations to give the women a position from which to speak.

What the examination of bisexuality tells us is that the women have a complex mix of essentialist and non-essentialist notions of identity. They hint at the idea of a true self that needs to be expressed through a label that they have yet to find. Being is more than just what one does. These women trouble the connection between gender and sexuality. They recognize that in conventional discourse, sexuality is organized around gender. They acknowledge this, at times resisting it and at times confirming it. Authenticity remains an important value for the women, although their task, as they see it, is to separate authenticity from the notion of stability. Their task is to come up with a way to make their identities authentic despite the fact that they lack stability, or the task in some cases is to show that there is stability despite fluidity in attraction. Since only two women have chosen to identify as heterosexual, it is safe to say that the majority of the women seek to maintain a non-straight identity. Bisexuality does not offer a solid enough ground for a non-straight identity. Its authenticity is often challenged and it is in some cases not considered queer enough, or queer at all. For this reason, the women have looked away from bisexuality as a viable identity outcome. If they do embrace it, they do so with many caveats, temporarily and in social interaction, in order to facilitate communication. They believe that there should be a label to which they will feel committed but they believe that they have not found it yet.

Chapter Four

Not Lesbian

The women in this study are mostly assumed to be bisexual, a label that they mostly reject for two reasons: the stigma associated with the identity and the fact that it does not align with who they believe themselves to be. Even though some of the women self-identified as lesbian prior to their involvement with men, the label of lesbian is also rejected, but for entirely different reasons.

Jennifer came out as a lesbian in her early 20s. She was politically active and involved in AIDS prevention work. She recalls that her parents were at first taken aback but then settled into acceptance of her identity, going as far as becoming active in Parents, Families and Friends of Lesbians and Gays (PFLAG), a support organization for friends and family members of gay and lesbian individuals. In her late 20s, while on a trip away from home, Jennifer met Tom. It was a friend who pointed out that Jennifer might be attracted to Tom. "I was embarrassed," she says, "that I hadn't noticed." Of the moment she noticed her attraction to Tom, Jennifer says she was "kind of horrified because that meant that everything was going to be different." At first, she tried to hide her involvement.

> I kept it a secret for a good while . . . [but] Once it became clear that this is not going to go away, and he was not going to somehow miraculously become a woman, and that I had to really stop being closeted, I started telling people.

Jennifer eventually married Tom, something about which she still expresses mixed emotions. She explains feeling "absolutely horrible about it . . . I often lie to people and say that we did not." She does not refer to Tom as her husband, preferring instead the term "partner." They have two children together. Today, Jennifer refrains from using the word *lesbian* to define herself.

> The label of lesbian was tremendously important. I identified as a radical lesbian, feminist and as a dyke and all of those terms were absolutely empowering and my complete identity. They were powerful, powerful important words in my life and there's nothing that remotely compares to that now. And lesbian also still counts as that core of my identity, so it feels kinda dishonest also to identify as anything else. Those terms still feel like important terms for me, but I don't use those terms because I think it's politically very damaging for the lesbian community.

She continues:

> I absolutely feel like I have lost my, I can't think of how to say it, I think I lost my right to claim my identity and the terms that feel right for me for defining my identity.

For Jennifer, the change to a partner of a different gender brings about a change in identity, not an identity that she considers her "core," but the identity with which she publicly affiliates. In the process of settling on an identity after involvement with men, Jennifer and other women like her not only negotiate what feels true to them, but also consider their obligations toward the lesbian community, a community to which they no longer belong.

INVESTMENT IN IDENTITY

Women who relinquish lesbian and bisexual identities do not differ significantly from women who do not in terms of their sexual milestones of first same-sex attraction, conduct, questioning, and most importantly identification (Diamond 2003). This is an important point, since the common understanding of lesbians who get involved with men is that they were insincere in their involvement with women, or that they are "fakers" or traitors, meaning that they were never "really lesbians."

How a lesbian identity is constructed prior to involvement with men affects the process of negotiating an identity after such an involvement. For the women in this study being a lesbian was an important part of their lives. Jennifer clearly articulates her investment in her lesbian identity, when she states: "My entire world and my entire identity, my work, was related to being a lesbian." Not only was Jennifer's lesbian identity important to her, but it was also an important part of her family dynamics.

> When I told my mother [about Tom], she got enraged. She said "I can't believe that you're doing this. I can't believe that you would do this. What am I supposed to do? I've got a p-flag meeting this week. Am I supposed to tell people? I can't go to work and tell people my daughter and her boyfriend are coming over for dinner. I would be humiliated to tell them something like that." [...] I very clearly had changed my mother's identity from the mother of

a heterosexual woman to the mother of a lesbian and then, here I was changing it again and she had no control over this aspect of her identity and it made her really angry because she had worked so hard to develop a positive identity as the mother of a lesbian and then I pulled it right from under her after all of that work.

Changing identities is stressful for the individual and generally speaking, people who are invested in a given identity resist changing it (Burke 2006).

Of the 14 women who previously self-identified as lesbian, none sought to retain the label while involved with men. The women in this study showed a great deal of protectionism toward the lesbian label. By distancing themselves from lesbian spaces, both physical and symbolic, they sought to preserve a sense of authenticity for those spaces. In some cases, the distancing was not of their choosing but in most cases, it was.

This protectiveness toward "lesbianism" manifested itself in two different ways. First, women exhibited a great sense of preservation toward the label of lesbian. They sought to keep the label untainted by removing themselves from under its umbrella, as in the case of Jennifer, although they still feel that the label captures something about their true identity. Second, they physically sought to preserve lesbian public spaces either by not occupying them anymore or at the very least, not occupying them with their male partners. Below, I outline the ways in which this sense of protectionism manifests itself in the process of (1) self-labeling or symbolic protectionism, and (2) navigating public spaces or physical protectionism.

SELF-LABELING

The process of choosing an identity label is by no means uncomplicated. None of the women with whom I spoke had an essentialist notion of what it means to be lesbian. They acknowledged variability in the lesbian experience. Despite this fact, the women, through their own experiences, sought to make room for an authentic lesbian experience that they no longer took part in. What exactly counted as an authentic lesbian experience, of course, varied from woman to woman, and sometimes varied within the same interview. Although the women were quick to explain that they knew of many lesbians who in the past had been or were currently in a relationship with a man, as mentioned, none of the women with whom I spoke identified as lesbian. I asked the women to explain this choice. If there is so much variety in the lesbian experience, why not continue to use the label?

Karen, who had previously identified as lesbian-queer, explains why she no longer identified as lesbian:

> 'Cause I'm a word-fiend, I like definitions to actually mean something and what I hate about labels for myself is also what I love about words, that they mean something and so, if I say tree you might picture a palm tree and somebody else may picture an oak tree and that's fine, just like when I say lesbian you might picture lipstick and curly hair and I might picture flannel or whatever and that's fine but, like we would all agree that a tree is a plant and it has roots, they go down in the ground, it takes up water, chlorophyll, whatever some kind of leaves or pine needles, brown and green, and so there's a general framework that everybody understands and I think it makes the word tree very powerful because it's universal, it's understood. There's variations on it but we know what it means, and what I would love about more flexible labels and just having a jillion labels for people's sexuality is also what I would hate if it happened to the rest of my words, like I want them to be kinda boxed in just a little bit so that there's a universal understanding.

Despite the fact that she mentions that many different types of "trees" exist, Karen considers her choice to be with a man as a difference of kind and not of degree, a universally understood difference. Just where that threshold of difference resides is unclear. The implication of Karen's reasoning for no longer considering herself a lesbian is that including her experience in the definition would make the definition itself meaningless. It would, in short, take power away from the word *lesbian* and this is clearly something that Karen does not wish to take part in. The fact that she offers no universally accepted definition of lesbian seems not to be of concern. The idea that keeping the label is detrimental is also echoed in Heather's statement. She states:

> I called myself lesbian for a while when I was, when I started dating my [male] partner. But I feel like that's not, I feel like I'm taking away somehow, from women who are exclusively with women, if I use the word lesbian.

As Heather's statement hints, the process of choosing a label is not an individually isolated process. Her assumption that she is "taking away somehow" outlines her feelings that her choice to keep the label does injury to women who do not have relationships with men. It seems that her very existence as a lesbian with a male partner is a threat to the legitimacy of a community that she cares greatly about. As a way to reconcile that, Heather, like Jennifer and Karen, gives up a label that she otherwise would want to use in order to preserve the authenticity of the community in which she used to belong.

Why would these women's choice to keep the label have any implication for anyone other than themselves? This is precisely because of the central role that the community plays in defining a lesbian identity. While involved with women, many of these women, like many other LGBTQ women have been bombarded by messages that their attraction and involvement with other women is a phase, or is otherwise not to be taken seriously. The idea that their attraction to women has somehow been viewed as a phase by others is a constant backdrop to their personal narratives. The women find themselves in a difficult place. On one hand, they need to make it clear that their attraction to women and the identities that they embraced previously were authentic, and not an experimental phase. They seek to make their previous choices authentic by confirming that they still find themselves attracted to other women. But they can only take this point so far. They refrain from continuing to identify as lesbian, in order to not fall into the stereotype that as Jennifer states: "all lesbians need is to meet the right man." Emily explains the situation as follows:

> part of my fear is that I think that, you know, to the ears of someone who doesn't understand what it means to be gay, I think that unfortunately that my experience makes the case that it's a choice and I know that, I think that, I know that's not true for so many people that I love. It's not, you know, so I do feel guilt about that. [...] I think my guilt is that it sounds like I make the case for choice, which I think is a very unhelpful, not even, it's a harmful experience to talk about to the biased ear, to the ear that wants to already reject and hate.

Jennifer remembers some direct feedback from friends:

> a couple of people specifically said I can't believe that you would do this, you know, this is exactly the stereotype that people have about gay people and specifically about lesbians and now you've proven them right and why not just not date this guy because it's really really bad.

Now involved with men, these women's fear is that they will further serve as an example of the impermanence or the inauthenticity of a lesbian identity. On the matter of becoming an example of choice, Jennifer explains:

> [...] I think it's too damaging. It fits into the stereotypes and I think does a lot of damage to the lesbian, gay, bisexual and transgendered queer movement too, there's so much of the civil rights activism that rests on, and I think inappropriately so, but that rests on we're born gay, we can't help it and my story flies in the face of that and I think would be used as an example by people in the ex-gay movement and in the, you know, people that want to change people's sexual orientation, who say that it's a choice, you can just choose something else, that I would be more fodder for that crap and I don't want to be that. So, in many ways, I think it's oppressive heterosexual society, you know, I talk about how I lost friends like that's, and I did, but I think I lost friends because of heterosexist oppression not because my friends were bad people although I'm pissed it wasn't, they weren't wrong about what image that creates.

When navigating the events following their partnership with men, these women are constantly working against the backdrop of their lesbian experiences having been a choice, and thus inauthentic. Their sense of personal authenticity is in conflict with a community's authenticity. On one hand, they work to explain that their involvement with women was not a phase. On the other hand, they work to not make the case for choice. This is an extremely difficult balance to maintain. In addition to maintaining this balance, the women distance themselves from the community, despite sometimes feeling profound loss. Karen puts it simply:

> I think the biggest hesitance is about like going back into the closet or whatever, you know, you've set up your community and then how does this affect the rest of your community.

Explaining her sense of loss, Tina states:

> You know, I love watching *The L-Word* and sometimes I feel like this isn't really your show anymore. You're not a lesbian anymore. I used to get *Curve Magazine* and I, you know, like you're not really a lesbian anymore so, I do, I feel like I kinda lost, part, being part of the club or whatever. And I feel like I lost that sense of solidarity.

Tina expresses her sense of loss but is inadvertently implying that there is an authentic lesbian who she no longer embodies. By placing *Curve Magazine* and *The L-Word* together and placing herself out, Tina is drawing a circle around what she considers to be "real" lesbian. She herself serves as an example of what is not real and through that process of exclusion, she inadvertently solidifies the notion of a real lesbian.

PUBLIC SPACES

Not only do some women relinquish the label of lesbian, but their desire to maintain an authentic lesbian community extends to avoiding lesbian public spaces, or at least, avoiding such places when in the company of their male partners. Riley explains this in terms of respect for a space that is made for a particular purpose. She says:

> I wouldn't enjoy them if I was with a man but also that I would feel, like honestly, being disrespectful, and I know that, you know, in theory that's ridiculous, but you know, I'm slightly sort of keeping it that way by respecting those kind of boundaries but there's something I kinda like about things being separate. I think it's important to have spaces that are not necessarily explicitly exclusive but that especially for, for the lack of a better word, minority groups, incredibly important, you know, and also I love feeling like there's almost this

like social service quality to my social behavior . . . there is something that's like, this isn't accessible for everyone.

Riley feels that bringing a man into a space that is considered lesbian would be disrespectful and thus she works hard to not sully the queer experience by presenting as heterosexual. Celia echoes these sentiments:

> I'm always concerned too, I want to remain respectful, like I won't be really affectionate with my husband in a gay bar. I do try to, you know, be respectful. And I don't go overboard, like I don't make sure that everybody knows he's my husband but at the same time, I don't deny that he's my husband. But, I'm conscious of that balance.

Celia wants to be respectful of the queer space she occupies. Somehow being affectionate with her husband is a sign of disrespect. One could assume that, according to Celia, it is not the affection that is disrespectful but the heteronormativity it signals. The relationship is a symbol of the structurally privileged social position of heterosexuality. I asked Meg about her experience of being in a space that caters to lesbian women. She explains:

> I think certainly, I felt uncomfortable dancing with him and being straight in a gay bar. But still if I were not with him I probably wouldn't have an issue with dancing with him in a gay bar, if he wasn't my partner.

The issue that Meg highlights is interesting. It is not the presence of a man in a gay bar that is of concern. Meg explains that she would dance with men at gay bars. The issue is bringing her heterosexual relationship into a gay bar, the same sentiment brought up by Celia. All three women show great reverence for a space that they consider serving a particular purpose, that of letting those who occupy it interact outside of the heterosexual gaze. The women perform the same level of policing of public spaces as they do of symbolic spaces. They physically refrain from coming into lesbian public spaces, thus protecting those spaces. They symbolically avoid such identity spaces, by refraining from identifying as lesbian.

COMMITMENT

Jennifer was very involved politically in the lesbian community. Her work and subsequent graduate studies all centered on her identity as a lesbian. But interestingly, it is precisely because of this investment, this commitment to and salience of the lesbian identity that she ceases to identify publically as lesbian. Jennifer's case highlights an interesting nuance, which has perhaps not been fully explored. Jennifer's political involvement and investment in the lesbian community may impact her desire to keep the label of lesbian as an important part of who she considers herself to be. But, this does not necessarily translate into publically embracing the lesbian label. In addition, it is clear that Jennifer's act to "give up" the label has nothing to do with a rejection of lesbianism, having gone through an experimental phase, or dissatisfaction with the lesbian community and identity. It is quite the opposite. Because she takes her commitment to the lesbian community seriously, Jennifer no longer applies the label to herself.

The women in this study do not necessarily have traditional understandings of sexuality. They admit that some lesbians are attracted to men. They acknowledge that one can be a lesbian and remain celibate. These women do not necessarily hold an essentialist notion of lesbianism but they do have a commitment to the lesbian community. These women themselves draw and redraw boundaries around their communities. It is not that these women have somehow accepted an essentialist notion of sexuality. They are aware that no real definition of lesbian exists. They also know, based on firsthand experience that a real lesbian community does exist. The women in this study occupy the uncharted territory between these two identity extremes; they are neither liberated by fluidity nor confined by tradition. Although they can no longer actively participate in the social aspects of that community, they still have a hand in shaping it. The last thing that these women desire is to have their experiences used as a platform to erode the sense of authenticity of the community that they cherish. Although concepts of community and identity are not monoliths, they do function as powerful forces in shaping people's lives. The concepts are fluid and socially constructed but they remain very real.

Regardless of how they feel personally, these women work extra hard to preserve what they consider a universally accepted notion of lesbian, even though they themselves acknowledge that their definitions are limited and few people actually live such categorically separate identities.

There are benefits to maintaining an identity, as identity change is often known to be stressful (Burke 2006). These women themselves could benefit from continuing to identify as lesbian, despite their involvement with men. They would not have to forgo relationships built on the basis of that identity. They could continue to watch *The L-Word* and buy *Curve Magazine*, in Tina's case. They could potentially remain part of the community that they cherish. Jennifer's mother could even remain in PFLAG. But they resist this. Instead they show great care for what it means to be lesbian, despite the fact that definitions are highly contested. They remove themselves because they do not want the label, and thus the community, to lose its power based on their experience. These women use an imperfect and at times conflicting definition of a real lesbian to protect a very real community.

Chapter Five

Not Straight

> So, when I first started dating the man that I'm with, I said if somebody, if it comes up, or whatever, I'm not gonna lie about who I am. (Sue)

The women who partner with men do not abandon their lesbian identity because they find it inadequate but do so as a way of returning authenticity to the lesbian community. Remaining "lesbian" at least to the public world, is not an option that the women embrace. Interestingly, straight, or heterosexual, is also not an option that they embrace. This is, however, for categorically different reasons. Two women in the study identified as straight and I will elaborate on their cases separately. The 30 other women did not, although they vary in the extent to which they share this fact openly with others.[1] In this chapter, I will explore why the women say they resist the straight label and how they challenge being assumed to be straight, an assumption that is at times inescapable. I will also highlight some of the reasons the women feel that the label of straight does not fit their experience despite the fact that their lives are seen as straight by others.

HETERONORMATIVITY

Heteronormativity refers in part to the underlying assumption that everyone is heterosexual. It captures the "taken-for-granted and simultaneously compulsory character of institutionalized heterosexuality" (Nielson, Walden, and Kunkel 2000). According to the women in the study, most people assume that they are straight. In fact, most people think most other people are straight. As Chloe, one of the respondents, stated "[…] there is the default of heterosexuality." The sentiment that there is a pervasive sense that everyone is straight was echoed in almost every interview. Nadia explained how unspoken assumptions lead others to conclude that she is straight. [...] new people that I meet, I think people just assume that I'm straight and don't necessarily know that about me, 'cause really it's been a long, you know, that was kinda a long time ago." This point is also made by other women, like Sue: "I think the people who just know me as being with guys, like they never think she's straight because they haven't thought anything else." The underlying assumption is that one is straight, unless one has some information to the contrary that one shares. The assumption of heterosexuality is so pervasive that, according to Claire, no one actually needs to verbalize it. It goes without saying.

Nadia's comment that her experience with women was "a long time ago" is different than what the other women expressed. It seems in this case that Nadia was trying to justify why others assume that she is straight. Nadia was not very bothered by that. She did not identify as such but she was ok when assumed to be straight. Jenny made a similar admission: "it's a default situation. It's not like a big deal." Jenny and Nadia both seem to forgive others for their assumption. Jenny, of course, is one of only two women in the study who actually does identify as straight. In a sense, straight being a "default situation" is more than just "not a big deal" for her. Being assumed to be straight is actually Jenny's goal. This is not a typical stance. As I will show in more detail later, the majority of the women who are assumed to be straight actually do take issue with it. Meg also seemed to understand why people would assume that she is straight but as the interview progressed, it became clear that she was actually quite bothered by this assumption.

> I think most people assume that I'm straight. I mean, I got a male partner. I have a kid. I'm pregnant, I think certainly they assume that I'm straight. [...] How do I bring up the fact that, like, I'm not really straight, you know, and my life is really straight. [...] I want to be like I'm not what you think I am. I'm not that person. [...] It feels like an odd and inauthentic thing to bring up later.

She, unlike Nadia, did not seem to believe that temporal distance from her experience with women should be a reason why people assume that she is straight. Similarly, Heather, who identified as bisexual, an unusual and complicated choice for the women in this study (see chapter 4 for more details), explained how she is read when partnered with a man: "When I'm dating a man, then they're not reading me as bisexual. They're reading me as straight."

Nadia, Meg, and Heather stressed that they are read as straight because they have male partners. Meg goes a step further and adds that she is read as straight because she is pregnant, which still implies the presence of a male partner. But Sue and Claire make a slightly different point. They call into attention the notion of heteronormativity. As Sue so clearly notes, her friends don't read her as anything at all and that in itself implies straight. The women's sexuality becomes unspoken. Being straight in a sense is being "nothing." Having a "sexuality" means being gay or lesbian, and in some cases, bisexual or queer. Lesbian, queer, and bisexual are "marked" categories, and heterosexual or straight, in that sense, is an unmarked category. What the women in this study have to contend with is this shift from being marked to unmarked. Before moving to the central theme of the women's desire not to be identified as straight despite having a male partner, I examine the case of the two women who do identify as such.

STRAIGHT

As mentioned, of the 32 women whom I interviewed, two identified as straight after their involvement with men: Jenny and Pam. Both women had identified as lesbian previous to their involvement with their male partners. At the time of the interview, I asked them how they identified.

> [...] At this point, this day, I would say that I'm heterosexual because I only date men. I really feel only attracted relationship-wise and physically to them. . . . But pretty much that's how I live my life, as a straight woman. I don't really even consider dating women. (Pam)

> I have chosen straight. 'Cause I'm not gay obviously, 'cause I'm not with a person of the same sex. (Jenny)

There is a slight difference between how Pam and Jenny seem to have come to their decision to identify as straight. Pam states that she is straight because she is only attracted to men and she is clear that she is not interested in dating women. Jenny, on the other hand, identifies as straight because as she put it, she is "not gay obviously." This difference shows the process by which these women have chosen an identity that feels right for them. Jenny spoke in terms of dichotomies, if not gay then straight. Pam spoke in terms of attraction. In a sense, Pam saw her involvement with men and her straight identity as something that follows her attraction. Jenny, on the other hand, seemed to see straight as something that has happened to her by virtue of her involvement with her male partner. Pam seemed to say that she is attracted to men and does not wish to be involved with women, and likes the label of straight, therefore she is straight. Jenny simply reasons that she is not gay, therefore she is straight. Jenny did not consider any other identity options.

Jenny and Pam, although their partners were aware of their previous relationships, did not discuss their involvement with women openly. But because heterosexuality is assumed of everyone unless proven otherwise, they don't have to do anything specific to be read as straight. Appearance is, as mentioned in chapter 3, an important part of presenting an authentic identity, and so, it is important to note that both Jenny and Pam are not in violation of any gender-normative markers. Pam has a child and Jenny is married to a man, which further informs why they are assumed to be heterosexual. The silence around heterosexuality and the assumption around its normality make it so all Jenny and Pam have to do is not tell anyone that they used to be involved with women. I asked Jenny if anyone in her current circle is aware of the previous relationship.

> Jenny: Right. Yes. You would be one of them.[2]
>
> Me: Ok. I'm one of them.
>
> Jenny: Really the only one.
>
> Me: Really am I the only one?
>
> Jenny: Except for my mom.
>
> Me: Ok. Alright. And your previous relationship, is that something that you share with people?
>
> Jenny: No.

Although neither Pam nor Jenny claim that their past identities were inauthentic or wrong, they are not open about their past. This is not a particularly difficult task for them. At this time in their lives, few people, if any, in their inner circle are aware of their involvement with women. Not only are many of the people around them not aware of their past, many of those who are aware of it are firmly invested in the women's straight identity. Jenny's parents are the only people in her circle who know of her involvement with her female partner. They are not divulging that information. They were not approving of Jenny's former relationship and are happy with and invested in the current one.

NOT STRAIGHT

Jenny and Pam's cases are not typical of the women in the study. The assumption of heterosexuality exists for almost all of the women but most also state that they want to find ways of challenging the assumption. This is the more difficult task. Juliana simply states:

> I feel like I can never ever be straight.

I will explore some of the reasons for Juliana's statement at the end of the chapter. The feeling of not being straight, despite involvement with a male partner, is expressed by many of the women in the study, like Celia:

> I don't want people to assume that I'm straight. Just because I'm here with a man, don't assume that I'm you know a 100% straight. [...] Straight does not fly with me, just because it's not how I see myself. To me, a straight person, you know, they can think a woman is beautiful but they don't have that emotional connection to women. I shouldn't say emotional connection, 'cause obviously with friends you would have an emotional connection, but I guess that appreciation for women on a physical and emotional level. My straight girlfriends they just have no concept of it. They've never thought about being with a woman. It just doesn't cross their minds and for me, that's just a daily part of my life. When I see a beautiful woman walking down the street, it's like "wow. She's so beautiful" or you know I'd really like to be her friend or it's just, it's different. I don't identify as straight.

What separates Celia from her "straight girlfriends" is her attraction to other women. But it was difficult it seemed, for Celia to articulate exactly what the key difference is between those who are straight and those who are not. She began by stating that the difference lies in making emotional connections with other women. She subsequently took that back. She then explained that she finds other women beautiful, although she stated earlier that her straight girlfriends also can find other women beautiful. She added that she can make a connection with women on a "physical and emotional level," but when she explained what she thinks about when she sees a beautiful woman on the street, she remarks, "I'd really like to be her friend," which does not necessarily speak to any kind of physical or sexual connection. Celia closes her statement by reiterating that she is not straight. And perhaps at that point, it was necessary to do so because she was not able to articulate any significant difference between herself and her straight girlfriends. Celia is married to her male partner and as I will discuss further below, I believe that her statement that she would "like to be her friend" speaks more to her status as a woman in a monogamous relationship than it does to her sexual attraction to other women. What renders her different from straight women, is the potential for sexual attraction to a friend. But saying that is not necessarily appropriate because she is married. Amy also considers herself different from straight women:

> My lifestyle really doesn't differ from any other straight woman that I suppose in the sense that, I don't sleep with women anymore, my relationships with women are, you know, platonic, are strictly platonic, [...] to me it seems dishonest to identify as only straight. It's not who I am, now, I mean, not that I feel a compulsion to let everybody know about it, but I certainly don't feel any kind of shame about it.

Not identifying as straight is a matter of honesty for Amy. She has chosen the more honest path, which is to acknowledge that she is not straight, despite what may appear to others. Abigail tries to be more specific about what exactly is the difference between her and a woman who identifies as straight:

> I mean, my experience for one thing. I guess that's a major thing for me and not just like the fact that I had those experiences but I guess of how they, how they changed me, like I still get little crushes on women. I guess that's probably different than a straight woman. I feel like, even though I'm not like plugged into queer culture nearly as much as [I] used to be, I still feel like culturally I'm different from a straight person in that I, like, I don't know what the correct word is, but I'm part of a different culture or I feel like I'm part of a different culture or something like that. I also think, in terms of my politics, I definitely take it very personally when there's any kind of challenge to gay rights or, or anything like that. [...]

Abigail's point about being culturally different is in itself different from Celia's point about attraction. Abigail explained that she still "get crushes" on women, so clearly attraction plays a role in her self-identification. But it is not just the fact that she has had experiences with women in the past that make her not straight. It is the fact that she is part of a "different culture." She felt part of this different culture, despite the fact that she is actually not "plugged in the queer culture." None of the other women expressed their identity so clearly in terms of cultural differences but in some ways, the other women did express their sense of loss of identity in terms of a loss of cultural connection. Tina, for example, explained that she felt that she could not watch certain television shows or buy certain magazines. What Abigail was able to articulate is that attraction alone may not be the sole difference between straight and non-straight women. By using the word "culture" she put her finger on the intangible "thing" that separates the two groups of women.

Straight is not an identity that feels right for the majority of the participants. In order to have an authentic claim on not being straight, the women name their attraction to other women as something that makes them different from straight women. Note however that Jenny and Pam also express having the potential to be attracted to other women, although they do not wish to have relationships with other women. Pam even admitted having had a sexual encounter with a female colleague in the month leading up to the interview, something that she only shared toward the end of the interview. However, their attraction is not something on which they base their identity. Jenny, for example, explains that her identity is based on the fact that she is in a relationship with a man. Relationships determine one's identity, she claimed. Identity is not something that one carries with one's self from relationship to relationship. This reasoning is not typical of the women in the study. For the majority of the other women, attraction is the basis for their non-straight identity, despite their relationships with men. Their potential for attraction to other women is what they believe separates them from "real straight women." But attraction is not something that is visible to others. The women have to come up with various different ways of making their attraction known to others.

ATTRACTION

Attraction is a key factor on which non-straight women build their claim to a non-straight identity. It is their attraction to other women and the potential for future relationships with women that makes these women think of themselves as non-straight. I use the term *non-straight* deliberately here, because the women vary in what non-straight identity they claim. Some argue that because of their attraction they are bisexual or queer. None, as mentioned previously however, identifies as lesbian.

> Because I'm still attracted to girls. Like a girl will still walk by and I will still think she's cute or sexy or attractive or whatever, so I guess that's why. (Mabel)

> I'll be vocal about it, like I'll be like "she's hot," you know, like, but I'll also be like "oh, he's hot. He looks good." (Juliana)

Mabel's attraction to women is not a tremendous source of discomfort for her, partially, I believe, because she is not in a monogamous relationship. The same is true for Juliana. Amy, on the other hand, is in a relationship, so the attraction to women is a bit more complicated to express:

> I'm still attracted to women. And if something were to God forbid happen to my husband, I would probably date women as well, again. I just happen to believe in monogamy right now.

Amy is not only stating that she is still attracted to women but she is also somehow explaining that she feels that attraction should lead to dating, for example. The reason she doesn't date women right now is because she is with her husband and not because she is not attracted to women. The only way she could entertain the idea of dating women is if she created a context in which her current relationship had ended. Emily and Ayana also found that in order to talk about their attraction to women, they somehow had to frame it in terms of the end of their current relationship. Although Hannah was also in a relationship, she is more comfortable stating that she has attraction to people other than her current partner. But to explain her point, she uses the example of a lesbian couple. In doing this, she is perhaps stating that attraction to women outside of one's relationship is not something that is associated with her past experience with women but is actually something that "most people" feel.

> I could still also be attracted to women. [...] Well, I don't think that, like a lesbian couple, you're in a monogamous lesbian relationship, I don't think they would say "oh, I'm not sexual anymore because I'm in a monogamous relationship" and stop identifying as lesbian and just say "I'm just in this monogamous relationship." So even if you are committed to someone, I think most people are still attracted to other people.

The level of comfort that Hannah seems to have with her attraction to women while in a relationship with her fiancé is not typical of the other respondents. Other women clearly felt some tension between attraction to people outside their relationship and their commitment to their partner. Abigail explains her attractions:

> [...] like I haven't really found myself having any real crushes on guys since I've been married but I have had some crushes on women.

Abigail is married to a man. The fact that she states that she is attracted to women and not men makes a point contrary to Hannah's. Abigail is stating that one is not necessarily attracted to people outside of one's relationship. The point that she is making is specifically about women.

Attraction is the main reason the women claim they do not qualify to be straight. But as the quotes above show, their monogamous relationships make the expression of that attraction, tricky. Following through with their attraction is not an option in their monogamous relationships because of "respect" for one's partner. To challenge assumptions of being heterosexual, they have other methods.

TELLING

> I think the bottom to the line is what does the fucking language mean to you. I think what does the language mean between you and your partner. Because again, out in the world, the world is not gonna know, unless you go everywhere telling it. (Claire)

Claire is mostly right. The world will not know unless the women take it upon themselves to tell. For those who wish to tell, many different matters have to be considered. Who to tell? How to tell? And when and to whom not to? The women struggle with these issues. I examine some of their mechanisms for telling and not telling below.

Who To Tell

> [...] not so much with family, like I don't so much talk about that with my family nor do I talk about that with my husband's family at all. But in terms of my friends, I don't let them forget that that is still an aspect of me, when I meet people, say at school, they all know, I'm open about it in my classes as well. If I have a story to tell and I happen to be with my girlfriend at the time, I'll say, you know, like when I was with my last girlfriend, you know, this is what we did and let them draw their own conclusions, like I don't, I don't hide that aspect of myself but I do, when it comes to family. Just because I don't think my husband's family could handle it. (Celia)

For Celia, the choice not to tell her husband's family seems to be an easy one. She justified that his family could not handle it. However, with her friends, she states that she is open and doesn't "let them forget." Celia felt different levels of obligation to her different audiences. Tina, on the other hand, felt that she could share that information with her husband's family. But, she nevertheless felt that she needed to check with him before she disclosed the information to his family. In her mind, he is implicated in the process and has a say in whether the information gets shared.

> If we went out with some of his relatives, and I asked him about it too, I said "do you mind if it comes up, if I clarify that I'm not straight." And he was like "I don't care. Whatever." I would never embarrass him or anything but it came up at one point at, oh, his brother's first wife realized she was a lesbian and they divorced and I was like "hey! I did it in reverse." You know.

The examples above are those of women who challenge assumptions of heterosexuality by disclosing their identity with a presumably heterosexual audience. Abigail touches on the issue of sharing this information with a non-heterosexual audience.

> She was lesbian and we met through work and we kinda just very gradually became friends and she assumed that I was straight and as we got to know each other better, as we got closer, I felt that it became clear to me that I had to set that straight because she would be talking about things, and kinda making assumptions about where I was coming from and so eventually I did tell her but it was something that I did put off because I felt like, especially in that situation, I was worried, [thinking] is this gonna be awkward or is she gonna take this the wrong [way], like I'm hitting on her, or something like that.

Abigail was worried that sharing her non-straight identity with someone who is herself lesbian may come across as an invitation of some sort. Again in this case, the audience determines the level and the process of sharing. Emily has a slightly different take:

> I definitely belong to some queer and ally organizations, and some of them, when you're in the group, you don't have to identify whether or not you're queer or ally. And there's times when I definitely want people to assume that I'm queer. And to me, that's still true, but I, but yeah, I guess, I would want, I don't want to say that I'm dating a man. And I'll be honest that's usually when there's someone in the room that I'm attracted to.

Emily draws attention to a slightly different process of sharing. In some cases, it is the male partner that is hidden, depending on the audience. For some women, managing their identity is not only about disclosing their non-straight identity to straight audiences, but it is doing the same with non-straight audiences and also perhaps hiding a male partner from a non-straight audience. Emily is dating a man, but the relationship remains fairly new. Perhaps if her relationship had some kind of requirement to be monogamous, Emily would not need to signal attraction and therefore would be less likely to hide her partner, "out of respect" for her partner, which some of the other women have hinted at. Different audiences require different levels of disclosure. These women are not uniformly out to everyone in their lives.

How To Tell

Even when the choice is made to share the information with friends, family, or strangers, the complicated issue is that of how exactly to share the information. As mentioned previously, there is an assumption of heterosexuality, so it is possible to imagine that those with whom the women interact assume that they are heterosexual.

If Asked

Answering questions about one's past and current attraction is potentially a risky endeavor, as it exposes the women to potentially homophobic reactions. As mentioned earlier in the chapter, there is a certain silence around heterosexuality, where the absence of an alternative leads to the assumption of heterosexuality. So, it is interesting that some women rely so heavily on others asking, when it tends to happen so rarely, if ever.

> At work, if they assume I'm straight or say something "oh, you're straight" or something like that, I would definitely correct them. (Alia)

> I have never once told anybody that I'm straight. So, I will correct anybody if they call me straight. (Mabel)

> [I] wouldn't lie. (Karen)

> It wasn't like I actually came and said, you know, I identify as bisexual. But, I never denied it either. (Celia)

> I wouldn't hide by any means but it just hasn't really come up in conversation. (Alia)

> If asked, I would certainly say, but you know, most people don't ask. (Amy)

> But, I'm rarely called upon, nobody normally asks. I just realized I sounded like a don't ask don't tell (laugh) and I don't mean to. It's not, it's not a situation where I would lie about it, if, if asked. (Abigail)

Recall Claire's comment that rarely does anyone ever actually call anyone else straight. Answering questions, when they are asked, is a well-intentioned course of action. But as it becomes evident by their own accounts, the women are seldom asked. As Hope clearly states, more often than not, "no one brings it up." Because of the assumption of heterosexuality, or heteornormativity, no one assumes that these women are anything but heterosexual. The women put the responsibility of "finding out" on others. This allows them to feel that they are not hiding anything but it also keeps them from having to disclose anything directly. The women, who wish to be seen as anything but heterosexual, have to find other ways of disclosing their identity, other than waiting to be asked. They have to find ways of bringing it into conversation.

Language

The women can't necessarily wait to be asked about their sexual identity, or they can, but the question may never come. Thus, the women have to find other ways of telling. Jennifer, for example, chooses to call her male partner, her "partner" as opposed to her "husband." By doing this, she invites her listeners to wonder why she has made that choice. This then brings her audience members to ask her the question that may otherwise go without asking. Notice, however, that in her last sentence, Jennifer separates herself from "gay people."

> I call [name] my partner, not my husband, and that stands out very very much to people and when they call him my husband, I correct them. And so then they say, "oh that's interesting, why don't you call him your husband?" And then I say "I don't think it's right that gay people can't get married and I can get married," and often it comes up in that context.

Beth takes a slightly more direct approach than Jennifer:

> Usually depending on the situation, I mean, we're talking about the very closed academic environment, and I never felt uncomfortable being like, like

as I got to know someone more, like being like well you know, like, he's the first guy I dated in 7 years.

Beth's beginning statement however shows that perhaps this is not necessarily how she addresses the issue in all situations. She explains that this type of direct sharing happens in a "closed academic environment." Karen, on the other hand, calls her male partner her husband and so she relies on another technique for disclosure. She works details of her experiences with women into conversations.

> I just talk about ex-girlfriends like I would talk about the fact that I'm a vegetarian. [...] it usually has come up in conversation just as in passing they mention something about their ex-boyfriend and I mention something about an ex-girlfriend or you know that has generally been my approach without hiding or making this big coming-out event. It's just thrown into the conversation with the rest of the conversation.

Similar to Karen, Celia works the information into the conversation.

> [...] like if somebody's saying well how did you meet your husband and or, how may people have you dated beforehand and I would, just if somebody asked me generally, about people that I had dated, I'd say, you know, oh, I dated this guy and this guy and then for a while I dated a woman, and they kinda look at me and I say "yeah, you know, it's not a big deal." Or if somebody, if there was a story about like you know, people will say "oh, have you ever been to, say Toronto, or have you ever been to this city." I'll say "oh yeah, you know, my girlfriend at the time and I, you know, we took a trip there." If it was relevant to the story I would just say it. And I don't try to, I don't try to force it into a conversation with straight people.

Juliana also chooses to talk about the past. She also shares that when she is in the presence of potential male partners, she simply shares her attraction to other women.

> You know, when I'm with a guy, I tell them that I like women, because I don't see myself as straight and I don't want them to perceive me as straight.

This is, yet again, an instance of how the audience affects how the process of sharing is handled.

Telling is not a straightforward process. For some women, finding instances where they can talk about ex-girlfriends, or deliberately calling their male companion their "partner" is an easy enough way to challenge assumptions. But telling is not always an option. One can foresee many instances where it would not be easy to work such information into a conversation.

NOT TELLING

The women vary in the ways they justify not disclosing their non-straight identities. The women fall into two groups, those who feel that they should be sharing the information and feel bad when they do not, and those who have made peace with the fact that not everyone will know their entire identity. Some argue that it is "weird" or "inauthentic" to bring up the fact out of context, while others state that not telling is sometimes the goal. It is just easier not to tell. And sometimes the women choose to take advantage of that. Some feel bad about it and others don't.

> I'm pretty sure she assumes that I'm straight and but I'm not gonna be like, because it's weird to just be like "well, by the way, I'm bisexual." Like, that's just, like, weird. (Juliana)

In this case, Juliana is talking about her mother. Short of having a classic coming-out moment, she doesn't seem to see any way of working the information into a conversation with her. It would be "weird" to do so. She then continues to explain that sometimes she decides not to share information, although she is unable to think of the reason:

> But like sometimes I do refrain from like coming out to someone that I perceive as straight because I don't know exactly why I do it, actually. I haven't thought about it, I don't know, I just test my ground sometimes, you know, I don't know I guess it just depends on how I feel with the person.

Although Juliana stated that she does not know why she does not share the information, the comment about testing one's grounds and feeling a certain way with her audience members leads me to believe that she is acting in a self-preserving way. She seems concerned about the reaction she might get from her audience. She seems worried about how she might be perceived. Holly also shares a similar concern:

> If they would say it outright, I would correct them. But I think most of the things people assume about your body, they don't actually verbalize. They just think them and there's no way to know for sure if they're thinking them, so you don't want to say anything and look crazy.

In the following quote, it is clear that Anne is really struggling with her choice not to share her non-straight identity with some people. She explains that she is doing so in order to avoid negative reactions. But there is clearly some ambivalence about the choice. This issue is not settled for her. She associates sharing with being an honest person.

> I like to live my life as an honest person so, if I feel like I'm not doing that, then, then I would feel guilty but then I guess if I think it's going to just negatively affect me and it really is how other people are going to perceive it and then how they're going to react to it. And I think I just have more growth to go in that area, trying to just let it go and people can either accept me for who I am or not and I think I still need to develop that more, you know like the sense of not caring what other people think about you.

Anne realizes that by sharing her non-straight identity she may be making herself vulnerable to negative reactions and she hopes that she can get to a point in her life where she will no longer care "what other people think." Karen also shares some of the ambivalence that Anne expresses:

> You know, what good can I do with disclosing and what am I going to bring on myself that is not fun if I disclose and weigh those things out. [...] may be because I just have more going on in my life I have less energy to be disclosing left and right to people who are just going to create yuck to deal with. [...] I go "I should be super-woman and I should say things that are uncomfortable to deal with and I should bring up these issues because they're important and like my silence is making it easier for them." And other days I'm like "the weight of the world is not on me and it's ok to have a regular day and I don't have to change people's minds about everything, or disclose everything about my life to try to bring up conversation with them," so I just take it one step at a time.

Similar to Juliana and Anne, Karen feels the pressure of being perceived negatively. She, however, seems to be a bit more comfortable with her decision to not disclose information about herself when she feels that it would take too much energy. Heather also expressed being torn between the desire to be visible and counter-cultural with the desire to be "kick back and enjoy a little bit." Heather also names a lack of energy as a reason why she chooses not to disclose:

> I don't know if it's because it's a man or not, I don't really care, you know, it bugs me that I am not as visibly counter-cultural or whatever because I feel like especially being wrapped up in grad school and law school, I don't have a lot of energy to do a lot of protesting and stuff so I don't have a lot of outlets for my political activism right now, and there's an area where it's not obvious but I also feel like, literally I feel like I don't care I'm tired, you know, I'm in my 40s, I'm probably at least half-way through my life, and I get to kick back and enjoy a little bit, if it takes being with this person, to help that happen, then that's what I'm gonna do.

Ayana shares a similar justification:

> His family, 'cause they're so freakin' religious, just irrational people, so, I'm not going to waste my time. I mean they are to the point, and that would go

with any extremely irrational close-minded people that I would encounter. I'm just not going to waste my time.

Ayana and Karen see certain instances of sharing as a waste of time, and so they refrain from sharing. Emily gives a rather different reason for not telling:

> If I was not with my current male partner and someone made some sort of assumption about my sexuality, I would question, I would challenge that, but I think that if I was holding hands with my male partner, and someone made an assumption about us being a straight couple, I wouldn't challenge that because that's what we look in the world.

According to Emily, her decision to not share has little to do with seeming weird, crazy, or even not wanting to put in the energy. Emily acknowledges that to the outside world, when she is with her male partner, she looks part of a straight couple. She seems to be hinting at the fact that she doesn't have the right to challenge the assumption because although she may not be straight, she is part of a straight couple. There doesn't seem to be much left to challenge. Abigail shares a similar ambivalence:

> I know that there've been other times. Just where it was less embedded in like a developing friendship and just someone making an off-hand comment then I would just say, "well, actually no. No. I'm not. I'm not straight. But I am married to a man." But then I feel like there've been some times when I just let it slide and obviously if I'm out [in public] and probably everyone I see is assuming that I'm straight, I just let that slide as well.

The point that Abigail makes echoes that of Emily. If a woman is in the company of her male partner, to whom she may be married, on what grounds can she challenge assumptions of heterosexuality? Telling and not telling require ongoing decision-making. Some women don't want to waste their time coming out as non-straight to people whom they assume will judge them negatively. Others don't want to "look crazy." Still others, like Emily, hide the fact that they are with men because they wish to remain attractive to potential female partners. Meg captures this difficult process of decision-making.

> Meg: I'm talking about my life, I feel, like to people who don't know me before I was with [husband], I feel like I wanna be like yeah but I mostly dated women most of my 20s.
>
> Me: And do you find yourself doing that?

Meg: Oh yeah. I totally do and then sometimes I find myself not doing it and feeling like, kinda conflicted about it.

Me: Yeah?

Meg: Like I'm exercising this privilege and really like being like kinda aware of it. So it's like really weird.

Me: So what, what goes through the mind, on the times when you decide you are going to say—

Meg: I don't know if I ever really decided. It's like a compulsion where I'm like "no I mostly date women" and then when I don't say I, I think "why didn't I do that," you know.

Me: Because sometimes you decide not to.

Meg: Yeah. Or I just don't do it. And then it feels like an odd and inauthentic thing to bring up later. Like how do I bring up the fact that, like, I'm not really straight, you know, and my life is like really straight.

Anne and Holly also bring up similar issues:

> Every time I use the term boyfriend, I feel strange about it. And like why am I saying that, and what am I doing? (Anne)

> No, it didn't feel good. I felt bad about [hiding her relationship with a man], I felt that I shouldn't, I felt guilty about hiding it. (Holly)

Not telling is in many ways not a particularly easy choice for non-straight women. Some not only feel that it lacks authenticity, but it also makes them share in the benefits of heterosexism. This is not necessarily a comfortable state for them, as the quotes above show. The women are, however, honest about the fact that they do sometimes indulge in the benefits that come with having a male partner. The guilt associated with that fact is almost always also present. I will elaborate on the issue of guilt and privilege in the following chapter.

WHY NOT STRAIGHT?

The women in this study do not want to be read as straight not necessarily because they do not "look" straight or "act" straight. But it is because despite the fact that they can be read as such, they do not want to be associated with what they understand "straight" to mean. The desire for these women not to be read as straight is not so much because they wish to remain political but because straight implies for them various traits that they wish to not take part in. Karen expresses this in very general terms:

> I'm straight, not really and it implies so many things that don't necessarily apply to me.

Riley, on the other hand, seeks to place herself outside of the straight "in-crowd":

> I don't really want to let them know, let them think that I'm like one of them.

Celia is a bit more detailed in her account of what she does not wish to take part in:

> I think just because society puts those expectations on, or puts those labels on you, versus when I was with a woman, it was, in a sense it was nice because there weren't the rigid gender roles, it was, you know, you did what you wanted because that's how you felt. Versus now, with [my partner], it's like I do these things because that's what the wife does and that's what the husband does.

To be straight, for Celia, not only implies having certain things, like a mortgage, car payments, but also being certain things, like a wife. It is the rigidity that comes with the label that she is trying to resist. Other women explain the rigidity associated with being straight not in terms of gender roles but in terms of a set of expectations.

> I don't think of love in like fairy tale terms. Or like my goals isn't like, oh let's get married. Like I'm not saying I'll never get married but you know or have kids but it's like not my agenda. You know, my top priority is like education, work, you know, and you know my family and my friends and then somebody else. Yeah and I guess straight is heteronormative, you know, and all the norms that come with it, like you know, like the way a family is supposed to look, you know, you have the nuclear family. [...] I wouldn't like conform to a lot of the norms. You know, but, at the same time, you're not forced to be like, be in a box. You know of how to act. And like, also like, you know like, I like to give pleasure too, you know, like with a guy, like, ok, not a lot of guys, there's some guys open to receiving, not all guys, you know, so I want to do that too. So, that makes me not straight too. You know, like I don't want to have sex in a typical way. [...] I don't want to have sex in a typical way. Like, yes I do like to receive, you know. But that's not all I want. Or how do I want, or how do you go about pleasing me 'cause like sometimes sex with guys like, fortunately I've had good experiences but some, like, just focus on like the penis into the vagina. And I, you know, like, with women, you do a lot more other stuff and I don't know, sometimes I like sex with women a little bit

> better. [...] You know, like in a straight relationship, a lot of guys assume that it's the penis in the vagina, but there's different ways to have sex and that's not the only way to get off. [...] there's like, seems like, well, at least for like my straight friends, like they have these rules for dating and like how they're supposed to act, like on the first date and on the second date and that just kinda bothers, like annoys me, you know, like, I don't know like, I don't know. I don't like that. (Juliana)

Juliana touches on everything that she associated with being straight from expectation of getting married and having children to a particular way of having sex. These are the things that "annoy" her and she resists them by being clear with her male partners that she is not straight.

> I think that there's some prices for [my partner] too. Like I get more pissed about him not doing laundry and not doing dishes than I would with a woman 'cause he's a man and "fuck you if you think I'm gonna do your dishes and I'm a servant because I'm a woman." Which my previous two partners didn't do dishes either. But, it was a different thing. (Jennifer)

As Jennifer clearly communicates, straight implies specific gender roles, rigid labels, and expectations to behave in a certain prescribed way, which may not always coincide with how one wishes to behave. It forces one to do "what the wife does." Juliana explains that straight is heteronormative. It comes with specific notions of what a family is "supposed to look like." It also comes with ways in which one has to behave in dating situations. Jennifer hints at a slightly different dimension, the power struggle within an intimate relationship and the division of household chores. For these women, straight implies traditional femininity, including modesty and knowledge of how to run a home. By stating that they are not straight, the women shrug off these expectations. They may be partnered and have sex with men, have children, dress in feminine ways, in some cases be married, be publically read as straight, but they are not straight. Because straight implies a certain lack of control over one's life. It lacks authority and is riddled with undesirable expectations and assumptions. I asked Meg to explain why she identifies as queer, as opposed to straight.

> I'm not really sure. Like I think part of it is defiance to like not, just because I look straight doesn't mean I am like, that's not, that doesn't define like who I embody. [...] Like when I was with women being queer was something I thought about a lot and now I don't, like I think about it more as a reaction than like as an identity may be. Like it was something I thought about and felt like it embodied me a lot when I was with women and now that I'm with a man now it's like this defiance, like I'm not what you think I am sort of thing, so it's a response or reaction to other.

Meg explains that her non-straight identity, in her case queer, is "defiance." The non-straight identity allows Meg and the other women to say exactly that: "I'm not who you think I am."

NOTES

1. A third woman, Nala, began the interview by identifying as "straight." Through the course of the interview, she disclosed that that may not be the "most honest" way to describe herself.

2. I am one of the only people aware of Jenny's history because we have been friends for many years.

Chapter Six

Hetero-cash

> I think because I'm like married to [husband] that people just make assumptions. […] (Nadia)

Research shows that those with social privilege often do not recognize the extent of the privilege (See Pratto and Stewart 2012). In general, women are likely more aware of their heterosexual privilege than men because of their status as women (Montgomery and Stewart 2012). According to Stein's 1997 study, women who once identified as lesbian and are now partnered with men are more critical of heterosexuality in a way that women who have always been partnered with men are not. This holds true for the women in this study as well. They are aware of others' perceptions of them, of the hidden benefits of heterosexuality, of the assumed normality of heterosexuality, and of the fact that the ways in which they get treated with their male partners would not necessarily be the way they would have been treated with their female partners. Marriage, one that is legally binding and recognized by the state, is associated with guilt about the benefits that it bestows. All the women are careful to stress that the social benefits of partnering with a man were not a factor in making the decision to leave their non-straight relationships.

Challenging homophobia is not an immediate indicator of being a member of the LGBTQ community. One does not have to be lesbian, bisexual, or queer to challenge homophobia. But the women nevertheless give this example as a way in which they work against heterosexism. This action is what many named as their way of setting themselves apart from their, at times, homophobic surroundings and assumptions of their own heterosexual identity.

Chapter 6
PRIVILEGE

Even the women who now identify as heterosexual are able to highlight the changes in their daily lives. For example, although Pam's church peers are not aware of her past, she expressed the ease of moving through her church community with her male partner:

> I want to feel comfortable at my church. I love the church I go to and I don't know if openly I would feel ok holding hands with a woman. And I feel ok about that. You know, I'm not going to over-think it like why don't I feel, I just do. And I'm good with that. I then, you know professionally, I just feel, like it just works out when I bring a date that's a guy. . . . I just want it to be easy in my life. And that feels easy.

Both Jenny and Pam stated several times that their current arrangements are much easier than their previous one. Their parents and support communities are invested in their straight identities. And there are many tangible benefits to being in a straight relationship, as Pam states:

> Right now I feel that I would want to be in another heterosexual marriage because there are a lot of privileges that go along with that, that you don't even think about. I like, I think I'd like that.

Sometimes the benefit of their current relationship translates into approval from family. Some family and friends make their feelings known only after these women begin relationships with men.

> There was definitely a lot of joy from straight friends and family since they felt that I was settling down, I think. [Laugh] The phase was over. (Celia)

Meg recalls her discomfort with the assumption:

> I think they feel, and not just like my parents, my extended family my grandma, grandpa, like we're talking and I'll be like "we're not in a monogamous relationship and I may still sleep with women" just because I want them to realize that this wasn't a phase and whatever.

Many of the women are aware of the benefits of being read as heterosexual. As Claire put it, "There's a whole level of heterosexual cash that you get, it's like a game. Yeah. It's like the heterosexual dollars are worth more." Many express guilt about sometimes letting the assumption of heterosexuality stand. Karen shares the following:

> It did bring up stuff that I don't I like sat down and thought about before, about who I disclose to and why. You know that there're whole categories of people

> to whom I don't disclose to and you asked if I felt guilty about my anonymity and I don't feel guilty about the anonymity that my husband provides me but yeah I probably feel guilty about times that I take advantage of that anonymity.

Other women also expressed feelings of discomfort when they withhold information.

> You know, watching TV with my husband, I might not make a comment about a woman, like I keep that to myself. Like last semester, I was a teaching assistant for gay and lesbian studies, so in that class, I felt like I was able to sort of explore these issues but when I came home, I didn't really talk to [my husband] about what went on in class. I just feel like it's become more compartmentalized, whereas before when I was, you know, openly bisexual, it's just like whatever, I didn't really think about it. But now, I think it's more of a respect thing for my husband. I don't want to throw it in his face. And also feeling guilty about maybe having an attraction to somebody else because it's, I'm in a monogamous relationship. You know, I'm a little more mindful of that. And I guess, you know, because you settle into married life. You have the mortgage. You have the car payment, groceries, like day-to-day life, those issues don't come to the surface as much as before you know, when I was living on my own and in school full-time, when I could really explore those issues and we do the couple thing, it's usually with, you know, a heterosexual couple and those issues just don't come to the surface, so I feel like it's sort of just, you know, my own personal struggle with it, I'm the only one who knows that I still do think about women. (Celia)

Celia brings up some important themes that many other women share. There is a sense of loneliness in Celia's statement. She is, as she put it, "the only one who knows" that she still thinks about women. Out of respect for her partner, her attraction to women has to be kept hidden or "compartmentalized." The issue of respect for one's partner, which other women also bring up, touches on the major issue that disclosure, or the decision not to disclose, involves consideration of not only the women themselves but their male partners as well. In addition, for Celia, monogamy, marriage, the mortgage, groceries, and car payments are all tied together. It seems that for Celia, heterosexual monogamy, in addition to the loneliness that it brings, is tied into day-to-day obligations.

CONTESTED PRIVILEGE

This privilege associated with heterosexuality is not available to all uniformly. Other identity components mediate the effect of sexuality (Steinbugler 2005). In the context of the United States, the effect of race on sexuality has been well documented (See Collins 2004). Emily, for example, does not associate ease of movement with her partnership.

> My current partner is also black and so, it just felt like way too much to bring him to, as the only guy and for sure, [...] but [also] the only African American person for sure. I just felt like it was too much.

She continues:

> being in a biracial partnership, we certainly still confront, probably more so now being with a black man, we've had people come up to us and be like "this isn't right." Yeah, we've been out before with my current partner, where, an older white woman just came up to me and told me that I was stupid and disgraceful for dating a black man.

Karen, whose partner is from Mexico explains how the benefit of being with a male partner is tempered because of the racism that her partner faces, and the scrutiny to which their relationship is subjected. Ramona, who identifies as "mixed" explains that she is assumed to be straight but she is also assumed to be white. This combination makes her privy to homophobia and racism that she assumes she would not be privy to if she were to be read as non-straight and a person of color.

MARRIAGE

Marriage as an institution that is currently not readily available in all states to non-straight couples, presents a difficult area of negotiation for the women in the study. The women are scattered along a spectrum of feeling about their decision to get married, ranging from a commitment to marriage equality to the desire to be divorced. Marriage to their male partners, in many cases, works as further proof of a straight identity that some seek to challenge. Tina articulates this point.

> [...] he proposed and I really didn't want to get married because I just, it's everything I'm against. I'm against this whole marriage thing, I don't think we should get married when all these gay people can't get married and I mean we're both members of the Human Rights, HRC, and we're both the faculty advisors for the gay straight alliance here on campus. You know we both believe in full rights for gays and lesbians and that's never been a conversation that we've ever had any problems with. [...] My friend, he and his boyfriend just went to California to get married and then of course the marriages, they I don't know, if they can't get married anymore and I don't know if they've decided they're gonna cancel now or what, but I'm God, I just feel so bad for him and then I feel so guilty that, I have the privilege that he doesn't, so, you know, I'm not part of that club anymore either. I don't know, so, I feel like yeah, like I kicked myself out of the club. [...] We got married [date] and I never meant to. It was a complete total accident, I swear.

The anguish that Tina feels at her decision to get married was tangible. She understood and was aware that her friend is not able to make a similar choice. What she decided to do in addition to being married is contributing funds to organizations that work for marriage equality. Meg explained that she had so much guilt over the advantages that she would receive as a married woman that she failed to acknowledge to herself that she truly desired to be married to her partner. It was for her an "important" choice.

> Meg: So, I think that was something that I really didn't realize when I got married that it's an important—I was like so uncomfortable just getting married and being married, you know like we had this party and we had, this, and I was so uncomfortable just like . . . it was fun and people gave us lots of stuff and it was a fun party but it was just like an uncomfortable—
>
> Me: Tell me about that. What was uncomfortable about it?
>
> Meg: I, maybe it was just because I felt like I was taking advantage of a privilege that I was able to take advantage of because I was with a man now and that people were celebrating this relationship that they would have not celebrated in the same way had I been with a woman. I don't know, I just remember like, I just did not want it to be about me, I think on some level I felt like this sense of like I was selling out my friends and like my community, that people thought that about me, you know, because I wasn't just like very, oh yeah I'm just getting married, I mean like you know obviously, like our decision to get married had a lot to do with convenience, you know like stability for a kid and legal protection and insurance and stuff like that, but I felt like I had to like really reiterate that part. [...] But [marriage] did mean something and like there's just a conflict, and I still feel it, now we've been married 3 years at this point, and I feel like there is less of that. I mean, certainly there is less, there still feels like there is that conflict, that discomfort.

Meg works to balance her guilt with the belief that marriage "did mean something." This is not only something that she had to contend with on the day of the festivities but something that she managed daily. Jennifer also expresses a struggle with similar issues:

> I'm still surprised that I'm in that kind of relationship. And there's so, so much privilege that comes with that word that, I'm really disgusted that I get to have, so I try not to use it, as much as possible, so most of the time when I use the term partner people assume that I'm a lesbian. And that feels right to me. Without being deceptive and without denying [my partner] in any way. It's the right term. [...] I mean, we did, I feel, absolutely horrible about it, still, but we

did get legally married. I often lie to people and say that we did not. So, I took on a lot of heterosexual privilege and we actually have talked many many many many times about getting divorced to get rid of that institutionalized privilege. But it's really really expensive to get divorced. [...] we were told that if we were not married, [my partner] would not be allowed in the room if there was any kind of medical emergency. Because he was not my partner, because he was not my husband. And that actually wasn't true, but we didn't know it at the time and got really scared and decided that that was a privilege that we wanted. [...] It really sucked, I mean it was very convenient and all that, but the minute we said it and they handed us the certificate, we both had this sinking feeling in our stomachs and regretted it, almost immediately. But, you know, then we felt like we had to and we didn't look into it until later. That night we sorta did, I don't think we talked about it that night, but the next day we started processing it and were horrified and they had said at the courthouse "you're now married in the eyes of God and in [the state]." And we were both really upset about that piece as well. And I think that's the piece we started talking about was, "wait you can't say that we're married in the eyes of God. You're the freaking state." [...] I feel certain that if we were in a different financial position, that we would have undone it by now and we always talk about when we say "what if we won the lottery and we weren't in $200,000 of debt anymore, what would we do?" and the very first thing we always say "well, I mean, after we get divorced, what would we do?" It's sort of a dream that we carry around.

Meg and Jennifer echo Tina's sense of guilt about marriage. Jennifer's desire to be divorced if only she had the money is one of the strongest negative reactions to being married. Others do not necessarily go as far as Jennifer to wish they could undo the process, but they do nevertheless feel conflicted about the benefits that come with being married to a man. Heather points to an ongoing dialogue in the queer community:

I feel guilty because I know gays and lesbians can't get married, not that everybody wants to get married. So, I don't know what will happen with that.

First, Heather explains that she feels guilty that she has the option of being married. She feels guilty because marriage has a privileged status in society. But not "everyone," that is not all gay and lesbian individuals view marriage as a political goal, although marriage is the most visible and heteronormative goal of the mainstream gay rights movement. Celia ties her conflict about the outcome of her own identity and her political commitment:

When I met [my husband], I just really had that connection with him and you know, knew that this was probably going to be the person for me and I really struggled with that, because I felt that if I presumed a relationship with him and it led to marriage, that part of me was gonna have to die, so to speak, that, I was never going to be able to, you know, have that experience again. On my wedding day, I actually felt that I had sold out. I felt that, you know, is that what this is truly about, is this about buying into that privilege? Is it because of, this is a safe decision? Is this because this is what's expected of me? So, through the last 10, 15 years, I always struggled, like am I really gay, am I bisexual? What am I?

For Celia, marriage creates a space of temporary identity confusion. Marriage does something beyond what a relationship with a man does. Celia also expresses guilt over the structurally privileged status of her relationship. Amy also brings up issues of guilt:

> I mean, is it even right for us to get married when there are still people who aren't allowed to. It was definitely, definitely a consideration. I didn't think about in terms of myself, though, I thought about it in terms of gay friends. I mean I didn't think, I didn't, I guess there was a fleeting thought of, you know, had he been a woman, I wouldn't be able to do this. I wouldn't be able to have sort of whirlwind legal marriage, if I had fallen in love with a woman. I did feel quite a bit of guilt actually, that like my best friend couldn't get these benefits either. So, we decided we would do it, but make sure that we would do whatever we could as, as citizens and sort of, in a small way, activists to make sure that others could get that, 'cause I mean he feels the same way I do. My husband feels the same way I do about gay marriage, you know. He feels strongly about it as well and so, we decided we would do it and then but still make it a priority to get something done.

Amy acknowledges her guilt but in implicating her husband's views of gay marriage, presents a scenario in which she and her husband become advocates for gay rights. So although their personal relationship is heterosexual, and she benefits from a system that her "best friend" does not have access to, she hopes to offset that by her activism.

Beth, who at the time of the interview was no longer in the marriage she describes, talks about the process of "downplaying" the importance of her marriage, in order to deal with some of the guilt she felt about participating in the institution:

> There were definitely times when I downplayed it like, "well, we got married because," and a couple of the reasons that we got married, frankly, are the financial benefits. He got free, like cheaper tuition 'cause like when I was a graduate student, like significant. I think he saved like almost $2000 one year, that second year that we were both in school in [city] when we were married, off his tuition because I was a full-time GA [graduate assistant]. You know, like our car insurance was cheaper. Everything was cheaper and we were in a position where we were like we need the help. And like we didn't pay for our wedding at all. Our parents paid for everything. My mother still reminds me about it once in a while.

Beth explains her choice to be married as a matter of economic necessity. That justification seems to somehow work out better than one that would state that she got married for "love" or "security." Nadia also highlights the economic need for marriage:

> I always say this to people, but, well, we got married for health insurance. I needed health insurance, so we got married and actually didn't tell our families for a while or our friends 'cause it wasn't like, I don't know, it just wasn't like a big deal to us in a way, then at some point my mom was going insane because I was living with someone in sin. She's very Irish and very Catholic. So that like made her crazy. So, anyway, finally we like told them "oh, we got married." [Husband's] mom was really mad because we eloped. My family was really mad because we didn't have a wedding because we didn't throw them a party. Like my mom was annoyed because we didn't get married in a church.

Stating that they got married for the financial benefits is one way that the women further separate themselves from the heterosexual female scripts regarding marriage. By boiling down marriage to a financially beneficial contract, the women solidify their claim that they are not part of the marriage-obsessed straight crowd but have made the decision in a rational way. Stating that the marriage was for money, rather than for love, or for the desire to have children, or for their parents' approval, seems to fit better into the women's sense of the "right reasons" to be married.

PARENTING

Marriage and parenthood are two institutions that some of the women had chosen to enter. Five women were parents and 11 were legally married to their male partners. In the women's narratives, both institutions serve as forces that they consider further "heterosexualizing." What the women indicate is that the sheer presence of children makes them read as heterosexual in public. Additionally, sharing parenting responsibilities with men is further associated in the women's narratives with their, in most cases, unwanted heterosexual lives.

The way the women manage their identity alone is different from the ways they managed their identity when in partnership with women and the way they have to manage it when in the presence of their male partners. Couplehood colors the ways in which gender and sexuality are visually performed. For four out of the five women who were parents at the time of the study, motherhood also affected the way gender and sexuality were performed. Despite the fact that lesbians can be, are, and always have been mothers, motherhood in itself is still a primarily heterosexual institution. Having a child, in many cases, distances these women further from a non-heterosexual identity (I use the term *non-heterosexual* here, because not all 4 women identified as lesbian). Jennifer shares the following story:

> I had an experience in the grocery store when [my daughter] was about 6 months old. It was in the frozen foods section and [my daughter] was with me in the cart, in the grocery store. And there was a very very cute lesbian in the isle with us and I did that whole, you know, gaydar signaling thing, where I looked a little long to be clear, to say that I see you, and I am like you or just to acknowledge each other and she got really really rude. And I realized that I didn't pass anymore, now that I had a kid. . . . It was very very devastating to me. I actually remember I cried for days afterwards. It was awful.

I asked Jennifer if it was possible that perhaps something she was wearing indicated that she was married.

> I don't think that that was it. We didn't have any kind of engagement ring or anything gold or anything that would look to me like a wedding ring. So, my assumption has always been, there may have been something else that cued it, that I just wasn't conscious of, but my assumption has always been that it was the presence of my daughter that did it. [...] Very interesting because it makes me feel choked up again. So, clearly it's not an entirely processed issue. It still clearly carries pain for me.

For Jennifer, the sole marker of her involvement with a man was the presence of her child. By having a child with her, Jennifer is even further read as heterosexual.

Some women name parenting with men as a mechanism that further places them in traditional heterosexual female roles.

> But, I think there is a very powerful, I think a lot of it for me is about parenting, 'cause there is so much societal support for women to be the primary parents and for men to help out and babysit the kids when the woman is away from home but there's a lot of parenting that feels very heterosexualized to me, that we have really worked, we've really tried to avoid and specifically not do, but, you know, he makes more than I do. He has a high school degree and I have a PhD and he makes more than me. And so, my job tends to come second or has in the past. Now that I have a full-time job with benefits, even though it makes less than him, I think we treat them equally, but, you know, there are those societal pressures and constraints but, other than that I'm not sure that there is a lot that's different. (Meg)

Throughout our conversation, Meg stressed how being pregnant almost automatically branded her as heterosexual. She is also aware not just of the visible changes of carrying a pregnancy, but the dynamics of parenting with a male partner, as opposed to a female partner.

> Certainly some parts of parenting with a man is really difficult in ways that I think would be different parenting with a woman, like that I've seen friends of mine who've had two women parenting together, parenting differently and things that you know feel like whoa, things that feel like, like gender stereotypes with men. I think that's awful true, with a lot of fathers, you know where they just don't seem to realize that even though they've been working all day in there, and they're tired and whatever, I've been at school or work, and then came home and dealt with baby and when they get home, I want them to take him to like, I need them to—you know I'm burned out. [...] With men that doesn't seem to be the same as my friends who have kids with women. And then I don't think it's a conscious thing, I just think that he's kinda obtuse about stuff.

The parenting hierarchy and the social support that comes with being a straight-appearing couple raising a kid, particularly a married straight-appearing couple raising a child, pushes the women further into being assumed heterosexual.

BECOMING AN ALLY

Montgomery and Stewart (2012) show that becoming a straight ally is a way for some heterosexual people to challenge heteronormativity. In a previous chapter, I showed how in order not to appear heterosexual, the women may try to make their attraction to other women known, they might wait to be asked about their identity, or they might work details about their previous relationships into conversations. Sometimes, the answer given by the women was not directly addressing my question. Although my question was specifically about how the women combat being read as straight and whether they challenge the assumptions of being straight, many women answered the question by stating that they would make a point to challenge overt homophobia. I include this tactic in this chapter because this strategy does not actually challenge the women's heterosexual identity. What it does do is allow them, in fact, the ability to speak out against homophobia, using their privileged position as members of the "sexual majority."

> Well, my first impulse is to say like, whenever I hear someone, like gay-bashing, or using the word gay derogatively, in a derogatory fashion, I always say something about it, or, bringing up those issues in my literature classes, like, why do we always read heteronormative books, right, like why is it always a man and a woman falling in love. But, nothing really beyond that. I don't know [...]. (Nala)

> When it comes to supporting the gay and lesbian rights and things like that, I definitely feel like I do. I definitely speak out against the, the ban on gays in

the military a lot. I speak out against that a lot because I have first-hand experience. (Alia)

They would say gay and queer and fag and stuff all the time. And I know they didn't mean anything by it but I would still harp on them and say there's no need for saying this stuff and it's really not funny. (Mabel)

Nala, Alia, and Mabel explain that challenging homophobic statements is a way to assert their non-straight-ness. The same is true for many other women in the study.

I just feel the need to butt in with my two cents when somebody makes some sort of narrow-minded comment. I do. [...] And I think that I would be a fake, I would be a fraud if I didn't stand up for it because I still feel it to be very much a part of who I am. (Ayana)

Ayana clearly states that challenging homophobia is "very much a part of who I am." Thus challenging homophobia is identity work. It is the way in which she "does" being not-straight. Same is true for Riley who feels that she would be "part of the problem" if she did not challenge homophobia.

If I'm in this strictly heterosexual setting with heterosexual people, and somebody says that something is gay or anything like that, I usually make a note, a verbal note of just like calling that out, whether it be in a joking way or sort of seriously like "how is that homosexual?" you know, like "really?" or if like somebody uses like faggot or dyke or anything like that like I don't let it slide 'cause I feel like that's sort of being part of the problem. (Riley)

Interestingly, Pam, who identifies as straight, is also adamant that she challenges homophobia.

You know, I still feel like if I heard somebody spouting nasty homophobic comments, I'm going to speak up. I'm gonna say "hey. That's not ok." And challenge that. It doesn't mean that I still don't care and that I don't love, you know.

Clearly, Pam's desire is not to use the challenge to assert a non-straight identity. In this case, challenging the comments is a way to protect the people and communities that she still loves.

For some of these women, confronting people about their homophobia is almost automatic. It is done without hesitation. But this is not always the case. Even challenging homophobia can be a thorny endeavor. Margaret explains her struggle with being assumed to be straight and challenging homophobia:

> When we're out together [with her boyfriend] and people assume that I'm straight, if I start to hear those old jokes around, you know just any kind of inference to, you know, I'm just ready. It does make me kind of like on edge, really, like where is this gonna go. Now it's harmless but where is it gonna go. You know, there's nothing derogatory being said, they're just joking around with each other, you know. You know, I don't want to say anything disrespectful, you know. Like, I'm not gonna be like "been there done that" or something like that in front of him. That's just disrespectful. You know, but I might say, how do you know some of us in this room aren't, you know, into dating the same sex, you know I might, you know, depending on what the environment is. Just, I don't have that much problem doing that. You know, and I'm not gonna worry about embarrassing him.

Margaret is not only referring to challenging homophobia but she is also touching on the bigger issue. She argues that when read as a straight person, she is likely to hear negative comments that may not otherwise be made in the company of LGBTQ people. It was Margaret herself who made a parallel between this feeling and the feeling she has as a white-appearing person of color:

> If I stuck up for black people, people would not assume that I was black but if I tell them that it's because I'm black that I'm saying this, [...] it's different when it's you and not you speaking for other people. I can sit out and call somebody out on something and not feel like they're going to turn on me and think that I'm, judge me or think of me negatively. If I say hey I'm black or hey I've been with women, that's like, it kind of, there's a part of you that feels like if I do that, then they can still invalidate what I'm saying 'cause it's just me. You know, as if I'm not enough. If I'm speaking up as somebody who's queer, if I'm speaking as somebody who has, you know, again, who has black blood in her, then they can negate that. [Like] I'm not holding them up to a moral standard, [but] that I'm being defensive.

Margaret's point is that if she challenged people on their homophobia or their racism, they could dismiss her comments as coming from someone who is too sensitive or can't take a joke. If people are not aware of her identities, she may seem like she is holding people "up to a moral standard." If she speaks up about her identity, her comments may simply be written off as another disgruntled person of color or lesbian who takes herself too seriously to appreciate jokes.

The legitimacy accorded to heterosexuality is not just a by-product of individual interactions (Jackson 2006). Despite it, the women in this study see their individual relationships and interactions as symbols of the legitimacy of heterosexuality and its privileged position with regard to other forms of sexuality.

Conclusion

Self and Story-Telling

Narrative analysis allows for the examination of subjective experience. Gubrium and Holstein (2009) state that "[In narratives] reality is about both the substance of the story and the activity of storytelling" (p.15). The purpose of the analysis of the stories of non-straight women who partner with men is not only to gain access to the ways in which they make sense of who they are but also as a way to zero in on what elements, people, and events, they perceive to be significant. Additionally, the narratives highlight the normative social assumptions underpinning the construction of sexuality. In the process of telling the stories of their involvement with men, the women in this study tell many other stories: stories of friendships, love, family, and community. The women present two main socially accepted notions about sexuality: a) attraction supposed to be limited to one gender and b) real sexuality is unchanging, thus change requires justification.

Some women interviewed make the distinction that attraction to both genders is not a problem for them. It is when they have to "go public" with their attraction and/or relationship that it becomes an issue. Some, like Jennifer, therefore wait to tell their friends and family about their involvement with men. For other women, attraction to men is in fact a problem for the women themselves. The attraction doesn't "make sense," and they find themselves wondering how it fits in with who they consider themselves to be. The women in this study want to maintain that both their attraction to women and their attraction to men were true reflections of who they are. Regardless of whether attraction to both genders is a "problem" for others alone, or for the women themselves as well as others, the women frame their narratives to address this concern.

One way to resolve this conflict is, of course, to claim that the attraction to women was misguided, fake, or a mistake, in a word, not a reflection of their "true self." But this strategy is not used by any of the women in the study. The women don't minimize their attraction to women. In fact, they never deny the reality of their attraction to women. Overall, instead of denying the validity of their previous attraction to women, they try to find other ways of solving this problem. They give their accounts legitimacy by invoking the classic coming-out story. They do away with the "phase" assumptions. They work to frame their attraction in terms of attraction to a person and not to a particular gender, thus minimizing the importance that gender plays in their attraction. They rely on conventional notions of love and attraction to justify the ways in which their partnerships with men were inevitable and "meant to be." These women tailor their narratives to address the many ways in which their claim to an authentic identity can be challenged.

The women recognize the importance of gender in organizing sexuality and sexual identity. This seemingly inevitable connection surfaces once again in the management of appearance. Through their appearance some women seek to make their choices seem legitimate so that their identities can be regarded as authentic. The ways in which dress is manipulated can be a powerful tool in the management of the relationships among sex, gender, and sexuality. Since this relationship is at the heart of the women's struggle, how they physically appear to others can have an important role to play in their identity work. Managing appearance is not an individually isolated process. Others, partners, and children serve as accomplices in the women's performance. Sometimes, the women and their partners are, in Goffman's terms, "teammates" in the management of appearance. When the women hint at the presence of an audience that watches their physical performance, they convey that they recognize the role that others play in validating their claim to a particular identity.

LIVING AUTHENTICALLY

There is no direct path between the women's dress and the identities they choose to embrace after becoming involved with men. Some women express no change in their dress, thus signaling that they are not changing into a different person. Some claim becoming more masculine either because they want to actively challenge the assumption that they are straight or they want to challenge the assumption of what "straight" looks like. The variety of strategies that the women use while managing their appearance does not lend itself to generalization. However, both the narrative of events and the narrative of appearance serve a similar purpose. Narratives of attraction and partnership not only communicate what happened, but more importantly they communicate who people are. In a society where biologically determined sexuality is the only "real" sexuality, having experienced a change needs justification. The story-telling choices these women make are motivated by their desire to be seen as authentic. They see their ability to present an authentic self as somehow evaluated by others, whether judged negatively or affirmed, even if they find themselves unable to articulate precise instances where they have received direct feedback about their given performances. What renders their performances authentic is in part contingent upon the audience itself. Performing an authentic self in the company of one's husband's family is different than doing so in the company of friends. The women, as shown in their accounts, don't consider this difference in performance as evidence of inauthenticity. They instead see it as a strategy for dealing with the many demands on their time. When they disclose that they don't share with their in-laws that they have been involved with women, some consider it "not worth it," for various reasons. They do not see it as a deceitful omission. Authenticity is the goal of a given performance, and each performance is also situation-dependent.

The analysis of how the women engage with the concept of bisexuality further illustrates how they organize and compartmentalize their desires and identities. Although the label of "bisexual" is one that many would associate with these women, perhaps surprisingly, they, in many ways, do not feel at home under the banner of bisexuality. The women consider the common perceptions of bisexuality to be a hindrance to their ability to fully embrace the label. Among the stereotypes associated with bisexuality, one that is most difficult to surmount is the assumption of non-monogamy. Non-monogamy implies a desire to/or a propensity to be involved with more than one partner at one time. The conceptual conflation of bisexuality and non-monogamy implies switching to partners of different genders, or going "back and forth" between the two genders. The trouble for the women in this study is that they wish to guard against this notion of "back and forth." They want to embody something more stable. In order to not be mistaken for someone who would go "back and forth," the women painstakingly express their commitment to their male partners. A legitimate claim to their identities, the women believe, is grounded in stability. They see themselves as authentic when they can also present their identity as stable. The label of bisexual doesn't offer them authenticity that is grounded in stability. The women make attempts to uncouple stability and authenticity but nevertheless fall back on the notion that real sexuality is a stable, unchanging one. They claim to be the "same person" as they were when involved with women, and they claim to be attracted to the "same qualities" in men and in women. Except for one woman, they also express blatant disapproval of non-monogamy. The label of bisexual is thus rejected.

None of the women in the study sought to keep their lesbian labels after becoming involved with men. This is true despite the fact that many women considered that identity to be a particularly important part of their lives prior to involvement with men. In the case of the label of lesbian, I propose that the women gave up their label because they feel a sense of obligation to the lesbian community. They gave up their label and their physical presence in lesbian spaces because they want to keep these spaces authentic. The women's experience, as they explain, can too easily serve as an example of "choice." The lesbian community as they understand it, is built around notions of essentialism, or being born a lesbian. The women fear that their experience will do harm to the lesbian community. Thus, their choice of identity after involvement with men is not about settling on a label that feels right to them alone, but is also motivated by the consequences of their choice for the lesbian community.

INVISIBILITY

Interestingly, the identity of "straight" or heterosexual is actively rejected by the majority of women in the study, though for different reasons. In part, being straight implies partaking in normative gender roles. Not being perceived as straight is both a goal and an ongoing task. Despite their efforts, the women are often read as straight, or as they themselves indicate, they are not read as "anything at all." They feel, as Heather states, "invisible." The women acknowledge that when they are assumed to be straight, in fact, it is because their sexuality goes under the radar. And so, during any given interaction, they have a choice to make. They can let assumptions stand, that is, they can choose not to challenge the fact that they are perceived as straight, which some do on occasion. Or, they work to not appear straight. The desire to not appear straight requires a particular set of negotiations. It requires that these women make choices about disclosure and challenge assumptions of heterosexuality, a task that proves to be difficult or nearly impossible at times.

At this point, some may wonder why the women in question do not solve their identity "problem" by identifying as queer. Some women do in fact use the term "queer" to describe themselves. But the term does not offer the majority of the women a way to express their identity in a way that feels authentic to them. Queer, typically a non-heterosexual umbrella term, lacks the stability component that some women seek to associate with their experience. It is a fluid category and one that is embraced by some specifically because it does not have any defined boundaries. The women, who reject the label "queer," do so for various reasons. For some women, like Alia, the word queer does not have a tangible meaning for the people around her, including her husband, friends, and family. Others, like Claire and Jennifer, feel that "queer" is a new word that they associate with younger women. They feel, in Jennifer's words, "too old" to use it. Juliana states that the word *queer* is associated with whiteness. She, as a woman of color, does not feel that the word is an adequate descriptor for her sexuality. Abigail, on the other hand, thinks of the word as too academic to be relevant in daily life. Nadia does not believe that the use of the word *queer* is an adequate way of fighting homophobia and she finds herself disagreeing with the politics that she believes are associated with identifying as queer. Clearly "queer" is not a possible solution for everyone.

Seven women do acknowledge that the term is the best fit for them, in the absence of something better. The women who do embrace the label, do so precisely because queer allows them to organize their attraction around something other than gender, thus addressing the fundamental "problem" of attraction to individuals of either gender. As Ari explains:

> Lesbian says woman-loving-woman, and queer says person-loving-person. I think that's the best way to capture it.

What attracts Ari to the label of queer is the fact that it does not limit the gender of individuals involved. The word *queer* has the ability to challenge the gendered organization of sexuality, more so than bisexual, as Heather explains:

> [...] part of why I like queer is because it's kinda non-determinative and all the other ones are specific labels about who you sleep with and I feel like there's so much more to sex and intimacy and who a person is than who they have sex with. And that's a really grotesque categorization of people. [...]

According to Heather, queer not only challenges gendered assumptions of sexuality, but it also moves sexuality beyond sex or "who you sleep with." This is a particularly useful way for Heather to maintain a non-straight identity, while also engaging in sexual behavior with a male partner.

Queer could be a solution to the problems that the women face, and clearly in some cases, it is. But in most cases, the word itself does not resonate with the women's experiences, for various reasons. It is either not one that they care to embrace—because they feel too old, or not white, or non-academic—or it is not meaningful to others with whom they interact. It is not sufficient to settle on a word that makes sense to the women themselves. It has to be a word that conveys to others the authentic, stable self that they seek to communicate. For many women, the word *queer* fails to do this. It also lacks any type of acknowledgement of a political commitment to contemporary, mainstream gay and lesbian rights social movements. Queer has risen as a response to identity politics and therefore it is often thought of as the anti-identity. But the women in this study, who did not identify as queer before partnering with men, feel a need to remain committed to the larger gay and lesbian rights movement, which in their mind is gay and lesbian and not queer.

THE SOCIAL

When lesbian, bisexual, and queer women partner with men, how they choose to sexually identify and label themselves is not an individual process but one that involves their perception of the feedback of others. Sexual identity is not just individual but it is also social. This limits the choices the women have when considering what they will "be" once they partner with men.

The key motivating factor in the ways the women construct their stories, tell their stories, and perform their given identities is the desire to be authentic. But what is authenticity? Who defines what is authentic? That varies. In the case of the interview itself, sometimes it is the interviewer who determines what is authentic. In the case of their daily life, authenticity is a negotiated process and implicated in interaction (Peterson 2005). When the women find themselves having to prove that they are living authentically, their claim to authenticity has already come into question. That is their point of departure. The work that follows is a series of efforts to restore that sense of authenticity. And this is done through clothing choices, story choices, and perhaps on some level, partner choices.

The story that the women tell is not only of "what happens when a lesbian dates a man," but it is the bigger story of continuously negotiating an authentic identity. Postmodern theorists have argued that as selves multiply, the desire or the ability to live authentically is diminished. But these narratives show neither that the desire to be authentic is diminished, nor that authenticity is any less valued.

The fluidity of identities have not affected the importance that people place on authenticity of identities. The participants in this study seem to indicate that they value authenticity and they accept that authenticity and stability are inseparable. Of course, the women shift in and out of assertions of this logic but the connection between stability and authenticity is the organizing feature of their narrative. It is one of the key reasons for their rejection of bisexuality, for example.

The women's identity choices are curtailed, on the one hand, by their desire to be authentic and, on the other hand, by their need to be understood by others. The women want to have their own claim to their identity recognized as legitimate. If they fail to make a legitimate claim, they will not be left without any identity, rather the gap will be filled at any given time, by identities inferred by people with whom they interact. The struggle is not between having an identity or being left without one. The struggle for these women is to have the identity that they claim be recognized by their audience as the best answer to the question "Who are you?" Each of these women is looking to be recognized as the authority on their own identity claim. In order to be the authority, they have to give the impression that they are "authorized" to be a particular performer. Notice that this understanding of authenticity gives the women some room to decide what performance they may be, or may not be, authorized to perform. They have some choices, but they do not have an infinite number of choices. They cannot decide alone what performance will be authenticated. This is a negotiation that they undertake with their audience. Some performances will be authenticated in some situations, like that of a daughter-in-law in the company of their in-laws. Some performances will not be authenticated, like Jennifer's attempt to establish a connection with a woman who she read as lesbian in a grocery store.

Everyone engages in authenticity work. But the visibility of authenticity work makes these women different from women for whom authenticity work is not made visible. A preoccupation with authenticity work colors most of these women's interactions with others. It influences their interaction with people whom they don't know, since they will have to choose whether to disclose their non-straight identity or not. It also influences their interaction with people whom they know, their partners, their children, their parents, and their friends. The difference between these women and women who have always partnered with men is that the former are chiefly aware of the work they have to do in order to be considered an authorized performer.

FLUIDITY

There are limitations to what identity can be embraced. The women in this study challenge the boundaries of some identities while working to preserve the boundaries of others. For them, not all identities are uniformly fluid. These women are not interested in stretching the boundaries of the lesbian identity. Recall Karen's comment about words losing their meaning. If the boundaries of the category of lesbian are stretched too far, Karen implied, it will lose its meaning. This is not something that these women are prepared for. They do not wish for the label of lesbian to lose its meaning. But they do not feel the same way about the label of straight. The women feel more empowered to challenge the assumptions of a straight identity. Fluidity is not present uniformly. All identity categories are not equally rejected. Some categories, precisely because of their social position, are more or less challenged than others.

Individuals may be afforded more room in the current social arrangement to challenge the meaning of given identities. They may wish to embody those identities in ways that challenge common understanding of those categories. In a way, they may be seeking to live more fluidly. But this fluidity is not present in all identities. Identities have different functions for individuals. The identity of lesbian is socially different than that of straight. It is much more important, and necessary, to build a community, whether political or non-political, around the label of lesbian than one built around the label of heterosexual. While it may be desirable to make the category of straight more fluid, to challenge it by not embracing the label, while also having a male partner, the same dynamics are not at play with the category of lesbian. The central difference between the two processes is the significance of community. All sexual identities do not hold the same social meaning, therefore the process of queering or the presence of fluidity is also not uniform between them. Nothing can really account for this difference other than the fact that the two categories, the two identities, are positioned differently within the social structure. As a still-stigmatized identity and as a community built on a stigmatized identity, the label of lesbian is not positioned equally to that of straight.

This is the story of how some women leave lesbian relationships and at times seek to re-mark their selves in order to fight the invisibility of living an unmarked sexual identity. The strategies they use to achieve this marked status are chiefly narrative. Narrative strategies of doing identity work are not limited to sexual identity. Using narrative strategies for identity work is a feature of postmodern societies, where individuals are living lives that are less bound to institutions such as family, religion, and work (Holstein and Gubrium 2000). The case of women who leave their lesbian relationship serves as a study of strategies that all individuals are using to a certain extent, as the resources provided for self-construction are made more contextual. Holstein and Gubrium argue that the self is "socially dispersed" (2000:215). The women in this study offer a way to conceptualize this social dispersion. The women who seek to not be read as straight do not have the same communal resources as those who want to be read as lesbian. They have for all intents and purposes stepped outside of a community that defines for them what it means to embody a certain identity. The identity into which they have stepped lacks the cohesion to provide them with new tools to define themselves.

Being authentic motivates individuals. Individuals also need to be understood by others. These statements seem obvious. But these two factors, as this study shows, actively mediate the identity work of the participants. This is a very different way of looking at the ways sexual identity shapes people's lives. Embracing a particular label is not only about putting a name on some "internal" desire. In fact, the choice of labels and the performance of a given identity are negotiated interactionally, with either a physical or an implied audience.

Bibliography

Ault, Amber. "Ambiguous Identity in an Unambiguous Sex/Gender Structure: The Case of Bisexual Women." *The Sociological Quarterly* 37, no. 3 (1996): 449–63.
Bamberg, Michael. "Who am I? Big or small—shallow or deep." *Theory and Psychology* 21, no. 1 (2010): 1–8.
Baumgartner, Jennifer. *Look Both Ways: Bisexual Politics*. New York: Farrar, Straus and Giroux, 2007.
Benwell, Bethan, and Elizabeth Stokoe. *Discourse and Identity*. Edinburgh: Edinburgh University Press, 2006.
Berlant, Lauren, and Michael Warner. "Sex in Public." In *Intimacy*, edited by Lauren Berlant, 311–60. Chicago, IL: University of Chicago Press, 2000.
Blumer, Herbert. *Symbolic Interactionism: Perspective and Method*. Englewood Cliffs, NJ: Prentice Hall, 1969.
Brekhus, Wayne. "Social Marking and the Mental Coloring of Identity: Sexual Identity Construction and the Maintenance in the United States." *Sociological Forum* 1, no. 3 (1996): 497–522.
Burke, Peter J. "Identity Processes and Social Stress." *American Sociological Review* 56 (1991): 836–49.
———. "Identity Change." *Social Psychology Quarterly* 69, no. 1 (2006): 81–96.
Butler, Judith. *Gender Trouble: Feminism and the Subversion of Identity*. New York: Routledge, 1990.
Callero, Peter L. "Role-Identity Salience." *Social Psychology Quarterly* 48, no. 3 (1985): 203–14.
Callis, April Scarlette. Bisexual, Pansexual, Queer: Non-Binary Identities and the Sexual Borderlands. *Sexualities* 17, no. 1/2 (2014): 63–80.
Capulet, Ian. "With Reps Like These: Bisexuality and Celebrity Status." *Journal of Bisexuality* 10, no. 3 (2010): 294–308.
Collins, Patricia Hill. *Black Sexual Politics: African Americans, Gender and the New Racism*. New York and London: Routledge, 2004.
Crawford, Mary. "Identity, Passing and Subversion." In *Heterosexuality: A Feminism and Psychology Reader*, edited by Sue Wilkonson and Celia Kitzinger, 43–45. Newbury Park, CA: Sage, 1993.
Crowder, Diane Griffin. "Lesbians and the (Re/De) Construction of the Female Body." In *Looking Queer: Body Image and Identity in Lesbian, Bisexual, Gay, and Transgender Communities*, edited by Dawn Atkins, 47–68. Binghamton, NY: Hayworth Press, 1998.

Davidman, Lynn and Arthur L. Griel. "Characters in Search of a Script: The Exit Narratives of Formerly Ultra-Orthodox Jews." *Journal for the Scientific Study of Religion* 46, no. 2 (2007): 201–16.

DeCecco, John P. "Confusing the Actor with the Act: Muddled Notions about Homosexuality." *Archives of Sexual Behavior* 19, no. 4 (1990): 409–12.

Diamond, Lisa M. *Sexual Fluidity: Understanding Women's Love and Desire.* Cambridge, MA: Harvard University Press, 2009.

———. "A New View of Lesbian Subtypes: Stable Versus Fluid Identity Trajectories over an 8-year Period." *Psychology of Women Quarterly* 29, no. 2 (2005): 119–28.

———. "Was It a Phase? Young Women's Relinquishment of Lesbian/Bisexual Identities Over a 5-Year Period." *Journal of Personality and Social Psychology* 84, no. 2 (2003): 352–64.

DiLapi Elena. "Lesbian Mothers and the Motherhood Hierarchy." *Journal of Homosexuality* 18, no.1–2 (1989): 101–21.

Dozier, Raine. "Beards, Breasts, and Bodies: Doing Sex in a Gendered World." *Gender & Society* 19, no. 3 (2005): 297–316.

Ebaugh, Helen Rose Fuchs. "Creating the Ex-Role." In *The Production of Reality: Essays and Readings on Social Interaction*, edited by Jodi O'Brian and Peter Kollock, 330–45. Thousand Oaks, CA: Pine Forge Press, 1988.

Entwistle, Joanne. *The Fashioned Body.* Malden, MA: Blackwell Publishing, 2000.

Esterberg, Kristin G. *Lesbian and Bisexual Identities: Constructing Communities, Constructing Selves.* Philadelphia, PA: Temple University Press, 1997.

Finkelstein, Joanne. *The Fashioned Self.* Philadelphia, PA: Temple University Press, 1991.

Fish, Stanley. *Is There a Text in This Class?: The Authority of Interpretive Communities.* Cambridge, MA: Harvard University Press, 1980.

Foss, Sonja K., Mary E. Domenico, and Karen A. Foss. *Gender Stories: Negotiating Identity in a Binary World.* Long Grove, IL: Waveland Press, 2013.

Foucault, Michel. *The History of Sexuality, Vol. 1.* New York: Random House, 1978.

Frie, Roger. "Identity, Narrative, and Lived Experience after Postmodernity: Between Multiplicity and Continuity." *Journal of Phenomenological Psychology* 41 (2011): 46–60.

Gagnon, John H. *An Interpretation of Desire.* Chicago and London: University of Chicago Press, 2004.

Garnets, Letitia D. "Sexual Orientations in Perspective." *Cultural Diversity and Ethnic Minority Psychology* 8, no. 2 (2002): 115–29.

Gergen, Kenneth J. *The Saturated Self: Dilemmas of Identity in Contemporary Life.* New York: Basic Books, 2000.

Gergen, Kenneth J., and Mary M. Gergen. "Narratives of the Self." In *Studies in Social Identity*, edited by Theodore R. Sabin and Karl E. Scheibe, 254–73. New York: Praeger Publishers, 1983.

Gleeson, Kate, and Hannah Frith. "Getting Noticed: Using Clothing to Negotiate Visibility." *Psychology of Women Section Review* 5, no. 2 (2003): 7–11.

Goffman, Erving. *Frame Analysis.* New York: Harper and Row, 1974.

———. *Stigma: Notes on the Management of Spoiled Identity.* New York: Simon and Schuler, 1963.

———. *The Presentation of Self in Everyday Life.* New York: Doubleday, 1959.

Golden, Carla. "What's in a Name? Sexual Self-Identification among Women." In *The Lives of Lesbians, Gays, and Bisexuals: Children to Adults*, edited by R. C. Savin-Williams and K. M. Cohen, 229–49. Fort Worth, TX: Harcourt Brace, 1996.

Green, Adam Isaiah. "Gay But Not Queer: Towards a Post-Queer Study of Sexuality." *Theory and Society* 31(2002): 521–45.

Gubrium, Jaber F. and James A. Holstein. *Analyzing Narrative Reality.* London: Sage Publications, 2009.

Hackl, Andrea M., C. Reyn Boyer and M. Paz Galupo. "From 'Gay Marriage Controversy' (2004) to 'Endorsement of Same-sex Marriage' (2012): Framing Bisexuality in the Marriage Equality Discourse." *Sexuality & Culture* 17 (2013), 512–24.

Halberstam, Judith. *Female Masculinity.* Durham, NC: Duke University Press, 2000.

Hawkes, Gail I. "Dressing-Up: Cross-Dressing and Sexual Dissonance." *Journal of Gender Studies* 4, no. 3 (1995): 261–70.
Heath, Mary. "Who's Afraid of Bisexuality?" *Gay & Lesbian Issues in Psychology Review* 6, no. 3 (2010):118–21.
Holliday, R. "Fashioning the Queer Self." In *Body Dressing*, edited by J. Entwistle and E. Wilson, 215–31. Oxford: Berg, 2001.
Holstein, James, and Jaber F. Gubrium. *The Self We Live By: Narrative Identity in a Postmodern World*. New York: Oxford University Press, 2000.
Israel, Tonia, and Jonathan Mohr. "Attitudes toward Bisexual Women and Men: Current Research, Future Directions." *Journal of Bisexuality* 4 (2004):117–34.
Jackson, Stevi. "The Sexual Self in Late Modernity." In *The Sexual Self: The Construction of Sexual Scripts*, edited by Michael Kimmel, 3–15. Nashville: Vanderbilt University Press, 2011.
———."Gender, Sexuality and Heterosexuality: The Complexity (and Limits) of Heteronormativity." *Feminist Theory* 7, no. 1 (2006): 105–21.
Johnson, Carol. "Heteronormative Citizenship and the Politics of Passing." *Sexualities* 5, no. 3 (2002): 317–36.
Juzwik, Mary M., and Denise Ives. "Small Stories as Resources for Performing Teacher Identity." *Narrative Inquiry* 20, no. 1 (2010): 37–61.
Kitzinger, Celia, and Sue Wilkonson. "Transitions from Heterosexuality to Lesbianism: The Discursive Production of Lesbian Identities." *Developmental Psychology* 31, no. 1 (1995): 95–104.
Kitzinger, Celia, Sue Wilkonson, and Rachel Perkins. "Theorizing Heterosexuality." *Feminism and Psychology* 2, no. 3 (1992): 293–324.
Krakauer, Ilana, and Suzanne Rose. "The Impact of Group Membership on Lesbians' Physical Appearance." *Journal of Lesbian Studies* 6, no. 1 (2002): 31–43.
Kraus, Wolfgang. "The Narrative Negotiation of Identity and Belonging." *Narrative Inquiry* 16, no. 1 (2006): 103–11.
Levitt, Heidi M., and Katherine R. Hiestand. "A Quest for Authenticity: Contemporary Butch Gender." *Sex Roles* 50, no. 9–10 (2004): 605–21.
Levitt, Heidi M., Elisabeth A. Gerrish, and Katherine R. Hiestand. "The Misunderstood Gender: A Model of Modern Femme Identity." *Sex Roles* 48, no. 3–4 (2003): 99–113.
Martin, Biddy. "Extraordinary Homosexuals and the Fear of Being Ordinary." *Differences: A Journal of Feminist Cultural Studies* 6, no. 2–3 (1994): 100–25.
Mason-Schrock, Douglas. "Transsexuals' Narrative Construction of the 'True Self.'" *Social Psychology Quarterly* 59, no. 3 (1996): 176–92.
McCormack, Coralie. "Storying Stories: A Narrative Approach to In-depth Interview Conversations." *Social Research Methodology* 7, no. 3 (2004): 219–36.
McFarland, Daniel, and Heili Pals. "Motives and Contexts of Identity Change: A Case for Network Effects." *Social Psychology Quarterly* 68, no. 4 (2005): 289–315.
McIntosh, Mary. "The Homosexual Role." *Social Problems* 16, no. 2 (1968): 182–92.
McLean, Kate C. and Marc A. Fournier. "The Content and Processes of Autobiographical Reasoning in Narrative Identity." *Journal of Research in Personality* 42 (2008): 527–45.
Mead, George Herbert. *Mind, Self, and Society from the Standpoint of a Social Behaviorist*. Chicago, IL: University of Chicago Press, 1934.
Montgomery, Samantha, and Abigail J. Stewart. "Privileged Allies in Lesbian and Gay Rights Activism: Gender, Generation, and Resistance to Heteronomativity." *Journal of Social Issues* 68, no. 1 (2012): 162–77.
Moss, Alison. "Alternative Families, Alternative Lives: Married Women Doing Bisexuality." *Journal of GLBT Family Studies* 8 (2012): 405–27.
Mullaney, Jamie. "Like a Virgin: Temptation, Resistance, and the Construction of Identities Based on 'Not Doings.'" *Qualitative Sociology* 24, no. 1 (2001): 3–24.
Nielson, Joyce, Glenda Walden, and Charlotte Kunkel. "Gendered Heteronormativity: Empirical Illustrations in Everyday Life." *The Sociological Quarterly* 41, no. 2 (2000): 283–96.

Ochs, Robyn. "Biphobia." In *Getting Bi: Voice of Bisexuals Around the World*, 2nd edition, edited by Robyn Ochs and Sarah E. Rowley, Sarah E. Bisexual Resource Center, (2009): 201–5. Retrieved June 12, 2014, http://robynochs.com/biphobia/.

Peplau, Letitia Ann, and Linda D. Garnets. "A New Paradigm for Understanding Women's Sexuality and Sexual Orientation." *Journal of Social Issues* 56, no. 2 (2000): 329–50.

Peterson, Richard A. "In Search of Authenticity." *Journal of Management Studies* 42, no. 5 (2005): 1083–98.

Pfeffer, Carla. "I Don't Like Passing as a Straight Woman: Queer Negotiations of Identity and Social Group Membership." *American Journal of Sociology* 120, no. 1 (2014): 1–44.

Plante, Rebecca. "In Search of Sexual Subjectivities: Exploring the Sociological Construction of Sexual Selves. In *The Sexual Self: The Construction of Sexual Scripts*, edited by Michael Kimmel, 31–48. Nashville: Vanderbilt University Press, 2011.

Plummer, Ken. "Queers, Bodies and Postmodern Sexualities: A Note on Revisiting the 'Sexual' in Symbolic Interactionism." *Qualitative Sociology* 26, no. 4 (2003): 515–30.

———. "Symbolic Interactionism and Sexual Conduct: An Emergent Perspective." In *Human Sexual Relations: Towards a Redefinition of Sexual Politics*, edited by Mike Brake, 223–41. New York: Pantheon, 1982.

———. *Telling Sexual Stories: Power, Change and Social Worlds*. London and New York: Routledge, 1995.

Ponse, Barbara. *Identities in the Lesbian World: The Social Construction of Self*. Westport, CT: Greenwood Press, 1978.

Ponticelli, Christy M. "Crafting Stories of Sexual Identity Reconstruction." *Social Psychological Quarterly* 62, no. 2 (1999): 157–72.

Potter, Andrew. *The Authenticity Hoax: How We Got Lost Finding Ourselves*. New York: Harper/HarperCollins, 2010.

Pratto, Felicia, and Abigail Stewart. "Group Dominance and the Half-blindness of Privilege." *Journal of Social Issues* 68, no. 1 (2012): 28–45.

Riessman, Catherine Kohler. *Narrative Analysis*. Newbury Park, CA: Sage Publications, 1993.

Rolley, Katrina. "Love, Desire and the Pursuit of the Whole: Dress and the Lesbian Couple." *Chic Thrills: A Fashion Reader*, edited by Juliet Ash and Elizabeth Wilson. Berkeley, CA: University of California Press, 1992.

Rothblum, Esther D. 1994. "Transforming Lesbian Sexuality." *Psychology of Women Quarterly* 18, no. 4: 627–41.

Rubin, Gayle. "The Traffic in Women: Notes on the Political Economy of Sex." In *Toward an Anthology of Women*, edited by Rayna Reiter. New York: Monthly Review Press, 1975.

Rubin, Herbert J., and Irene S. Rubin. *Qualitative Interviewing: The Art of Hearing Data*. Thousand Oaks, CA: Sage Publications, 2005.

Rust, Paula. "Two Many and Not Enough: The Meaning of Bisexual Identities." *Journal of Bisexuality* 1, no. 1 (2001): 31–68.

———. "Coming Out in the Age of Social Constructionism." *Gender & Society* 7, no. 1 (1993): 50–77.

Ryan, Maura. "The Gender of Pregnancy: Masculine Lesbians Talk about Reproduction." *Journal of Lesbian Studies* 17, no. 2 (2013): 119–33.

Schecter, Ellen. "Women-Loving-Women Loving Men: Sexual Fluidity and Sexual Identity in Midlife Lesbians." Unpublished Dissertation, Fielding Graduate Institute, 2004.

Schrock, Douglas P., and Reid, Lori L. "Transsexuals' Sexual Stories." *Archives of Sexual Behavior* 35, no. 1 (2006): 75–86.

Schwalbe, Michael, and Douglas Mason-Schrock. "Identity Work as Group Process." *Advances in Group Processes* 13 (1996): 113–47.

Shively, Michael G., and John P. DeCecco. "Components of Sexual Identity." *Journal of Homosexuality* 3, no. 1 (1997): 41–48.

Simon, William, and John H. Gagnon. "Sexual Scripts: Origins, Influences and Changes." *Qualitative Sociology* 26, no. 4 (2003): 491–97.

Stein, Arlene. *Sex and Sensibility: Stories of a Lesbian Generation*. Berkeley, Los Angeles, London: University of California Press, 1997.

Steinbugler, Amy C. "Visibility as Privilege and Danger: Heterosexual and Same-Sex Interracial Intimacy in the 21st Century." *Sexualities* 8, no. 4 (2005): 425–43.
Stets, Jan E., and Peter J. Burke. "Identity Theory and Social Identity Theory." *Social Psychology Quarterly* 63, no. 3 (2000): 224–37.
Stone, Sharon Dale. "Bisexual Women and the 'Threat' to Lesbian Space: Or What If All the Lesbians Leave?" *Frontiers: A Journal of Women's Studies* 16, no.1 (1996): 101–16.
Stryker, Sheldon, and Peter J. Burke. "The Past, Present and Future of an Identity Theory." *Social Psychology Quarterly* 63, no. 4 (2000): 284–97.
Stryker, Sheldon, and Richard T. Serpe. "Identity Salience and Psychological Centrality: Equivalent, Overlapping, or Complementary Concepts?" *Social Psychology Quarterly* 57, no. 1 (1994): 16–35.
Swidler, Ann. *Talk of Love: How Culture Matters*. Chicago and London: University of Chicago Press, 2001.
Turner, Ralph H. "The Role and the Person." *American Journal of Sociology* 84, no. 1 (1978): 1–23.
Umberson, Debra. *Death of a Parent: Transition to a New Adult Identity*. Cambridge, MA: Cambridge University Press, 2003.
Vannini, Phillip A. "The Changing Meanings of Authenticity: An Interpretive Biography of Professors' Work Experiences." *Studies in Symbolic Interaction* 29 (2007): 63–90.
Vannini, Philip, and Alexis Franzes. "The Authenticity of Self: Conceptualization, Personal Experience, and Practice." *Sociology Compass* 2, no. 5 (2008): 1621–37.
Walters, Suzanna Danuta. "The Power in Choosing to Be Gay." *The Atlantic*, June 3, 2014. http://www.theatlantic.com/health/archive/2014/06/whats-wrong-with-choosing-to-be-gay/371551/.
Ward, Jane. "Gender Labor: Transmen, Femmes, and Collective Work of Transgression." *Sexualities* 13, no. 2 (2010): 236–54.
Ward, Jane, and Beth Schneider. "The Reaches of Heteronormativity: An Introduction." *Gender and Society* 23, no. 4 (2009): 433–39.
Watson, Janet. "Bisexuality and Family: Narratives of Silence, Solace, and Strength." *Journal of GLBT Family Studies* 10, no. 1/2 (2014): 10–123.
Weiss, Jillian T. "GL vs. BT: The Archeology of Biphobia and Transphobia within the U.S. Gay and Lesbian Community." *Journal of Bisexuality* 3, no. 3 (2003): 25–55.
Wells, Kathleen. *Narrative Inquiry*. New York: Oxford University Press, 2011.
Wilson, Elizabeth. "Deviant Dress." *Feminist Review* 35 (1990): 67–74.
Woodward, Sophie. "Looking Good: Feeling Right—Aesthetics of the Self." In *Clothing as Material Culture*, edited by Susanne Kuchler and Daniel Miller. New York: Berg, 2005.
Ybema, Sierk, Tom Keenoy, Cliff Oswick, Armin Beverungen, Nick Ellis, and Ida Sabelis. "Articulating Identities." *Human Relations* 62 (2009): 299–322.
Young, Rebecca M., and Ilan H. Meyer. "The Trouble with 'MSM' and 'WSW': Erasure of the Sexual-Minority Person in Public Health Discourse." *American Journal of Public Health* 95, no. 7 (2005): 1144–49.
Zaylia, Jessie L. "Toward a Newer Theory of Sexuality: Terms, Titles, and the Bitter Taste of Bisexuality." *Journal of Bisexuality* 9 (2009): 109–23.

Index

appearance, 11–12, 13, 14, 17, 18, 20. *See also* dress
attraction, 12, 17, 24, 25, 26, 34, 37, 40, 51, 54, 77; to men, 6, 7, 8, 44, 47; to women, 9, 49, 50, 51, 52, 56, 67
audience, 18, 53, 54, 55, 56, 57, 78
authenticity, 24, 35–36, 81, 82; desire to be, 78, 82, 84; lacking, 28, 29, 30, 41, 57, 60; of community, 39, 40, 42, 44, 45; of identity, 2, 7, 8, 18, 31, 47, 78, 79, 80; of performance, 16, 82; of space, 39, 80. *See also* bisexuality

biological determinism, ix, x, xii, 25, 78
bisexual, xi; assumed to be, 35, 79; identifying as, 24, 46
bisexuality, 23, 24, 36; inadequacy of label, 26; lack of authenticity, 27, 28, 29, 30, 31
butch/femme, 17, 18

choice, xiii, 3, 28, 29; to be with men, 3, 5; to be with women, 42
coming out, xiii; reverse, 2
community, x, xi, 15, 66, 84; belonging, xi, 12, 13; gay and lesbian, 23, 26, 27, 38, 40, 42, 43, 44, 45, 80; heterosexual, 21
cultural connection, 50

desire, xii, 3, 7, 12, 26, 79

dress, 12, 13, 15, 21; change in dress, 11, 14; normative gender, 12, 19

essentialism, 31, 36, 39, 44

family, 4, 38, 53, 66; parents, 17, 18, 37, 48
femininity, 14, 15, 62; non-traditional, 20; normative standards of beauty, 13; resistance to standards of beauty, 22
fluidity, 25, 28, 44, 83, 84

gender, xii; and sexuality, 12; as basis for attraction, 7, 25, 26; categories, 25, 34; non-conformity, 12, 19, 20; normative markers, 47. *See also* dress
guilt, 60, 65, 66, 70; about marriage, 71

heteronormativity, 43, 45, 46, 55, 62; challenging, 22, 74; heterosexism, 65
heterosexual, xi; assumption of being, 19, 22, 45, 46, 47, 54, 59, 66; identifying as, 13, 47, 50, 66; label, 45, 61, 62; relationship, 7
heterosexuality as default, 15; benefits of, x, 7, 8, 15, 43, 60, 65, 66, 67; challenging assumptions of, 48, 59; gendered expectations, 62
homophobia, 7, 19, 65, 68; challenging, 74, 75, 76

identity, 44, 55; based on relationships, 50; marked, xiii, 13, 19, 46; as performance, 16, 82; personal vs. social, 15; sexual, ix, x, xiii, 3, 18, 24, 84; stability of, 28, 30; unmarked, xiii, 46; as work, 5
invisibility, xiii, 19, 80

Kinsey scale, 1

labels, 23, 31, 34, 35, 36, 39, 40, 84
lesbian, xi, 14, 18; label, 43, 83; perceptions of bisexuality, 27; spaces, 11, 39, 43

male partner, xiii, 22, 55, 56, 59, 67; unlike other men, 8; transgender, 21
marriage, 10, 49, 52, 65, 67, 68, 69, 70, 71, 72; working for equality, 69
monogamy, 52; non-monogamy, 28
motherhood, 72, 73. *See also* parenting

narratives, xi, 3
non-straight identity, xiii, 22, 36, 51, 53, 57

parenting, 73, 74; children, 47. *See also* pregnancy

phase, 5, 40; bisexuality as, 28. *See also* scripts
political allies, 28
postmodern theory, 82
pregnancy, 46, 73

queer, xii, 30, 63, 80–81; community, 29, 70; culture, 50; perspective on marriage, 70; space, 43

racism, 68, 76

scripts, xi, 1, 3; accident, 6, 8; classic coming out, 2, 3, 7; cultural, 1, 9; gender-blind, 7, 8; just-happened. *See* accident; love, 9, 10; person discourse, 25, 26; phase, 3, 5
sexual categories, xiii, 1, 15, 23, 25
sexuality, ix, xi; as drive, 6; behavior, xii; orientation vs. preference, ix; social assumptions of, 77
stereotypes, 2; of bisexual people, 27, 32
stigma, xiii, 19, 24, 32, 37, 84
story. *See* scripts
straight. *See* heterosexual

visibility, 15, 58

About the Author

Ahoo Tabatabai is an assistant professor of sociology, in the Psychology and Sociology Department at Columbia College. She earned a PhD in sociology and an MA in women's studies from the University of Cincinnati. Her areas of teaching and research interest include gender, sexuality, and narratives of identity.